'Slices from a Life' is a collection of the autobiographical anecdotes which Sh. Abhimanyu Unnuth, the famous Mauritian writer and colummist, had undergone from his childhood till the present day, spanning his entire life and career. These anecdotes were published as 'Monday Views of Abhimanyu Unnuth' under the weekly series titled 'Slices from a Life' in the popular Mauritian newspaper. The author says that some of his publishers in New Delhi had been persistently requesting him to write his memoirs for the sake of the Indian readers as they had been very popular with the Mauritian population, who owe their heritage and legacy to mother India literally.

DIAMOND BOOKS PRESENTS

Srikantha Arunachalam
- Treatise on Ayurveda 295.00

David Servan Schreiber 'Gurier'
- The Instinct to Heal 195.00
  (Curing stress, anxiety and depression. without drugs and without talk therapy)

Swati Lodha
- Why Women Are What They Are . 195.00

Osho
- Nirvana : The Last Nightmare 195.00
- Yoga - The Alchemy of Yoga. 150.00

Dr. Bimal Chhajer
- Zero Oil Thali 150.00
- 201 Tips for Diabites Patients 150.00
- 201 Diet Tips for Heart Patients 150.00
- 201 Tips for Losing Weight 150.00

Joginder Singh
- For a Better Tomorrow 150.00
- Jokes of Joginder singh (I, II) 95.00

Pandit Atre
- Soul @ Universe.Com 75.00

M.G. Devasahayam
- India's IInd Freedom an Untold Saga 195.00

Vandana Verma
- Lovely Names for Babies (Male & Female childs) 95.00

BOOKS ON HINDU MYTHOLOGY

Prafull Goradia
- The Saffron Book 150.00
- Anti Hindus 150.00
- Muslim League's Unfinished Agenda 150.00
- Hindu Masjids 195.00

Dr. Brij Raj Kishore
- Essence of Vedas 195.00

S. N. Mathur
- Gautam Budha 295.00
- The Diamond Books of Hindu Gods and Goddesses (4 Colour) 295.00

B.K. Chaturvedi
- Shiva Purana 95.00
- Vishnu Purana 95.00
- Markandeya Purana 75.00
- Bhsvishya Purana 75.00
- Narad Purana 75.00
- Kalki Purana 75.00
- Linga Purana 75.00
- Devibhagwat Purana 75.00

Dr. Kiran Bedi Presents'
- Shadow in Cases 225.00
- Rest in Piece 95.00

LITERATURE

Rabindranath Tagore
- Boat Accident (Translation of नौका डूबी) 95.00
- Inside Outside (Translation of घरे बाइरे) 95.00

Iqbal Ramoowalia
- The Death Of A Passport 150.00

Ed. Rajendra Awasthy
- Selected Gujrati Short Stories 95.00
- Selected Hindi Short Stories 125.00
- Selected Tamil Short Stories 95.00
- Selected Malayalam Short Stories 95.00
- Selected Punjabi Short Stories 95.00

GREAT PERSONALITIES (BIOGRAPHY)

Meena Agarwal
- Indira Gandhi 95.00
- Rajiv Gandhi 95.00

Anuradha Ray
- The Making of Mahatma 95.00

Prof. Gurpreet Singh
- Ten Masters (Sikh Gurus) 60.00
- The Soul of Sikhism 95.00

B.K. Chaturvedi
- Messiah of Poor Mother Teresa 60.00
- Chanakya 95.00
- Goddess Durga 95.00

S.P. Bansal
- Lord Rama 95.00
- Gajanan 75.00

Dr. Brij Raj Kishore
- Ram Krishna Paramhans 95.00

Purnima Majumdaar
- Yogiraj Arvind 75.00
- Neel Kanth (Lord Shiva) 95.00

Dr. Bhwan Singh Rana
- Swami Vivekanand 95.00
- Chhatrapati Shivaji 95.00
- Bhagat Singh 95.00
- Maharana Pratap 95.00

Mahesh Sharma
- Dr. A.P.J. Abdul Kalam 95.00
- Sonia Gandhi 95.00
- Atal Bihari Vajpayee 95.00
- Lal Krishna Advani 95.00

Books can be requisitioned by V.P.P. Postage charges will be Rs. 20/- per book. For orders of three books the postage will be free.

DIAMOND POCKET BOOKS

X-30, Okhla Industrial Area, Phase-II, New Delhi-110020, Phone : 011-51611861, Fax : 011-51611866
E-mail : sales@diamondpublication.com, Website : www.fusionbooks.com

Slices from a Life
(Memoirs of a Great Author of Mauritius)

ABHIMANYU UNNUTH

DIAMOND BOOKS

No part of this book may be reproduced or transmitted in any form or by any means, electronic or mechanical including photocopying or recording or by any information storage and retrieval systems without permission in writing from **Diamond Pocket Books (P) Ltd.**

© Author
ISBN : 81-288-1009-X

Published by : **DIAMOND POCKET BOOKS (P) LTD.**
X-30, Okhla Industrial Area, Phase - II
New Delhi - 110 020
Phone : 011-51611861 - 865
Fax : 011-51611866
E-mail : sales@diamondpublication.com
Website : www.diamondpublication.com

Edition : 2005

Price : Rs. 125/-

Laser Typesetting : R. S. Prints
✆ : 26857488

Printed by : Adarsh Printers,
Navin Shahdara, Delhi-110032

Slices from a Life
by Abhimanyu Unnuth

Contents

During Dire Straits	7
Passport for Music Land	10
Gift From Kins	13
Donation Donated	16
The Source of a Trilogy	19
Month Without Pay Day	22
Fête Cabs and My First Earning	25
Punishment Without Tears	28
Made in England	33
The Taste of the Roasted Hare	37
The Days of Ajanta Arts	41
The Expensive Coin	45
Encounter with the Wind	49
Berries Sweet and Sour	53
Amongst the Don Juans	57
Monday Was Not a Holiday	60
The Fast U-turn	63
In the Midst of Poets and Politicians	67
My Addiction for Comics	70
Memento of Unemployed Days	73
Winning the Race and Losing Face	76
Visa for Cinema	80
The Film Without an 'End'	83
Of Death	86
The Hot Groundnut	89
The Fear	93

Back to the Canefield	97
The Day I Left the Canefields	101
When I was Lured to Steal	104
Lust for Books	107
The Rehearsal	110
The Aroma of Grilled Maize	113
Stone Shoes	117
Hospitality Vended	120
The Big Save	123
My First Pair of Shoes	127
Days of Toys	131
The Outcast That I Am	134
Money Bearing Tree	137
Shares of the Offerings	141
The Colour of White	145
The Nasty Trick	149
The Game	153
Looking for the Swami	157
My Friend Gaffoor	160
The Prediction	164
Slices from a Life	168
My First Protest	171
A Dream Created	174
Sold at Five Cents	178

During Dire Straits

Moment of one's past, be it a bitter one or one full of bliss, it comes, sometimes to our mind swiftly and as alive as when it occurred. This is reminded to us either by seeing an object or a scene. There are instances when this remembrance comes to us by hearing a voice, a piece of music or by a certain smell. There might be more factors that take us down the memory lane and plunge us in nostalgia. Moments of my past have been reminders to me in so many ways. Every *Sankranti* celebration reminds me of my mother's death. My mother died on a *Sankranti day*. Like in so many houses in Mauritius, my mother, as tradition wants it, used to prepare *Khichri* on that auspicious occasion. Up to now every 14th January takes me back to the time-tunnel where scenes of my mother's struggle are as though rewinded to me.

Last year, it was again the *Sankranti* festival. I was reading Oscar Lewis' book "*The Children of Sanchez*" which was given to me by Sir Kher Jagatsingh. I was in my room simultaneously thinking of the poverty in Latin America and my own days of sufferings when I got the smell of *Khichri* coming from the kitchen though it hadn't the same aroma of my mother's *Khichri*. I was instantly taken back to my childhood days. In those days of dire straits our main food, at home, consisted of sweet potato, maize and breadfruit, from the huge tree in our backyard. Whenever my mother bought a kilo of "manioc" she would boil half of it and consigned the other half under the earth to keep it fresh for weeks. *Sankranti*, then, was a public holiday and was celebrated throughout the island with great religious enthusiasm and cultural devotion. I was back home after a match of "*Kabaddi*" with my friends, a game which has now gone into oblivion, like so many of our ancestral heritage, the flying of kites, the "*Gooli danda*" and others. It was my days of primary school. Both our house and the kitchen were of thatched roofs. Part of the walls of our house of Ravenalle and Raffia and part of dried sugar cane straw, covered with a mix of white swamp soil and cowdung. Like most of villages' huts of the period.

Rice, in those days, were sold on ration-cards and as it was also expensive, my parents couldn't afford it. My mother was in the habit of buying maize with its stalk to have it cheaper. She would grind it in the *Jaffa*, the stone-grinder, with the help of one of my two unmarried sisters. She then separated it in two parts by sieving it. The finer grain she kept for "*Litti*", the thick *paratha* and the thicker grain to cook as rice. The maize "*Litti*" was my father's delight when served with "*Brede Chowrayi* and *Coriander chutney*". The prosperous days of my father were over. He was unemployed and most of the time ailing.

Prior to the unfair trial of which he was victim my father owned acres of land, coach and car. I hadn't seen those days. My mother with her slim and frail looking body had an inner strenght. Agile and tireless she was able to breed two cows and half a dozen goats and was tireless in providing them with green fodder. Her name Soobagya, meaning the lucky one, was for her the irony of fate, and yet she would never allow her evershining smile vanish. When there would be no poultry and eggs to sell and provide food to her family of seven members she would boil "manioc" for our dinner to be taken with tea. And when even "manioc" was not available she told us stories and sang Bhojpuri folksongs, one of her favourite "*Gham ke maral passina bahé koré ke maral khoon*" which she had learnt from her immigrant brother, who much later became the protagonist of my trilogy. My mother's songs and stories made us forget our hunger and we used to listen them until we were asleep. Along with my two younger brothers I shared a thin mattress covered with gunny and had gunny sheet to cover in cold nights. Our hunger too fell asleep to wake up in the morning. The smell of *Khichri* took me back to the days of my mother.

I was tired after a struggling match and wholly drenched with sweat. My mother didn't allow me to enter the kitchen without having a wash but the aroma of the *Khichri* was so inviting and so full of temptation that even someone who had just taken his lunch couldn't resist it. My two unmarried elder sisters have never succeeded in preparing so tasteful a *Khichri* despite several attempts. I said to my mother—

Slices from a Life

"I'm very hungry."

I was asked to have patience because the cooking wasn't ready and to have my wash first. I had no alternative than to rush to the tap under the mango tree. Even there the pleasant smell was reaching my nose. After some splashes over my half naked body I was on the verge to move to the house when I saw people entering our front yard. It was my eldest sister with her husband, her mother-in-law and her two kids coming from Olivia, Bel Air, where she was married. My sister's mother-in-law was a good storyteller and I was always happy on her rare arrivals.

I was indeed very happy until I heard my mother saying to my second sister—

"They are five, the *Khichri* will not be enough."

It was known to me that coming to Triolet from Olivia one had to leave very early in the morning.

My elder sister said to my mother—

"They surely have left Olivia with only their morning tea."

I saw my eldest sister from Olivia entering the kitchen and said to my mother—

"The children are very hungry."

It was already lunch time. I looked at the *Degchi* still on the fire place which by no means could have contained the rice and split-peas mix for more than seven persons. When my mother left the kitchen along with my eldest sister to meet our relatives before serving them food I opened the small cooking pot on the table. It contained some "*Doorimaye*", the boiled split maize of the previous night. When my mother re-entered the kitchen to serve lunch I said to her:

"Mummy, don't you have some "*Doorimaye*" left? It was so tasty. Please, Ma, I'm very hungry."

My mother looked at me with a melange of pain and relief in her eyes.

Passport for Music Land

The house of one of my publishers, Shrimati Sheela Sandhu, in Lajpat Nagar, New Delhi, has been a place of peaceful stay for me. An abode of great relief after going through the streets of a city increasing in pollution, Sheela ji's house has, on several occasions, given me the bliss and tenderness which only a decision above that of writer and publisher could provide. There are so many reminiscences of that magnificent house that it's impossible for me to speak of them all in this column. On one occasion, my wife Sarita also had the privilege of sharing the pleas of the hospitality of which she still says that we were never aware, not even for a single minute of being away from our family.

Sheelaji was so fond of Sarita that during our whole stay, she didn't fail to ask everyday, of her choice from breakfast to dinner. And it was after her very shy request that she ordered Choté, her young cook, for specific preparation.

It was the house where several great writers both from India and abroad have got the opportunity of staying. I had the privilege of meeting quite a number of top Indian authors in the house. Sheelaji was not only my first publisher but also my guide and well-wisher. It was in 1969, when I was a primary school teacher and I don't know how, I dared to submit my handwritten manuscript to the greatest publishing house of India. It was that of my first novel *Aur Nadi Bahti Rahi*. I did it, perhaps in the same way, as I used to send my poems, short stories and articles to the top Indian magazines, that is, without being sure of being accepted.

It was to my great amazement when, only two months later, I received a reply which I didn't dream of. I was as happy as a child on the occasion of the Christmas. My first novel was accepted to be published by the most prestigious publisher. The letter had the signature of the Managing Director, Sheela Sandhu. Thus, it was the beginning of a non-stop literary trek. Among so many unforgettable moments of Sheelaji's company, I am coming here with two reminiscent slices.

The gentle lady used to look after me as though I was a child and would never allow me to go outside without a sweater or coat. Having known of my easy going habit, she would advise me to be serious at times and to have my programmes well scheduled beforehand. She said to me one day:

"Please Abhimanyu, try to reply letters in time. Even when you happen to write back, it's only a few lines. Like a telegram. How can you manage to write novels?"

Her second remark was:

"Spare yourself from being too forgetful. You are not yet a philosopher."

And to what degree this was true, let the following event speak of itself. It was a very cold afternoon. I was on my way to Lajpat Nagar after meeting with my publishers and editors of the Daryaganj area. When I reached home, I noticed that my passport, which I had taken with me for banking purposes, wasn't with me. I had only my traveller's cheque book in the envelope. In my free time, I had done a bit of shopping at Janpath, so I emptied my travelling bag and the two shopping bags containing the purchased goods but couldn't find the passport. I lost all my wits and turned pale. Seeing me worried, Sheelaji came to me and said:

"It seems that you have forgotten something."

"My passport!"

"I'm not surprised, not at all. It was expected from you."

After a little pause, she said:

"Try to remember all the places where you opened the bag containing the envelope."

"I opened it only at the American Express Bank."

Suddenly, I was reminded of the taxi. During the trip back, I had opened my traveller's bag to transfer in it some of the articles from the two shopping bags. In that process, I had taken out a few things from my traveller's bag. I told Sheelaji immediately:

"Now I can remember. I had taken out my passport from the bag and had placed it on the back seat where I was sitting."

She, very promptly, asked me:

"Where did you hire the taxi? Was it in the streets or a taxi stand?"

I knew the place. When I told my host that it was a taxi stand near the Cannaught Place, she, without losing a second, started dialling. The first two dialling brought nothing. From the third one we were told that a driver had left in custody a black leather folder with a Mauritian passport inside to the supervisor of the stand.

Sheelaji asked her driver to take me to the said taxi stand. Before leaving the house, I informed my host that the passport holder had in its hiding part two notes of hundred dollars.

Lamenting for my fate Sheelaji said:

"You will get your passport at all cost but for the money, let's hope that the taxi driver is as forgetful as you and as careless."

At the taxi stand, it was a *Sardar* who handed the passport holder to me. I opened it in front of him and looked inside the two pockets. Disheartened I said to him:

"*Sardarji* there was two hundred..."

"Ay you! You got back your passport, thank God. Ok?"

Thanking God, I took my seat in the car and said to myself:

"Two hundred dollars for a passport! Quite expensive."

Two hundred dollars meant a lot to me but getting back my passport was a great consolation.

The second unforgettable moment at Sheelaji's place happened the next day. We were having our breakfast when my host wanted to know my programme of the day and asked me:

"What are you doing tonight?"

"I'm waiting for a call from Rajendra Yadav. He will ring me after talking with his wife Manooji."

"Is it for a dinner?"

"I think so."

"This you can keep for later on. Why don't you go for a concert by Pandit Ravi Shanker? I have already booked for two tickets. Sandhuji will accompany you."

I was thrilled by it. Attending a live concert by the great maestro of *Sitar* was a long cherished desire of mine. It was fulfilled when at night in the company of Mr. Sandhu, I attended the grand recital. The atmosphere was serene and full of a certain divinity. Sitting in cross-legged posture on the mat for hours wasn't easy but the sweetness of the music made it a must and easy as well. Fortunately we had our seats very close to the two great musicians of the world, Pandit Ravi Shanker and the *Tabla* genius Allarakha. It was a real feast by two supreme musicians of the time when the climax of *Sitar* and *Tabla* reached to a crescendo of harmonial dexterity. My losing of the two-hundred dollars was converted into an invaluable and unforgettable moment of my life.

Gift from Kins

I was working as a teacher at that time and had just started getting published in Indian magazines. Some of my friends were very pleased when they went through my stories but there were others who didn't like them. They were those who refused to believe that I was the writer of those stories which I was at that time signing with the pseudonym of "Shabnam". Even when later on I gave up the pen name a few of my friends went up saying that there was another Abhimanyu Unnuth and being his namesake I was declaring his writing as mine. Those who happened to accept the stories to be mine didn't fail to brand my stories as plagiarism. Others would say that my language was rather Urdu than Hindi because of my free use of Urdu words. I paid no heed to all the calumnies against me and I continued my literary trek. The acceptance came much later when my writings started appearing in the most prestigious Indian Press like "*The Times of India*" and the "*Hindustan Times*", but still there were some people with better background of the language who never ceased with their below-the-belt attack.

The biggest blow of them all occurred when my first novel "*Aur Nadi Bahti Rahi*" was published by Rajkamal Prakashan, the topmost publishing house of New Delhi. It was in 1970. When this first Mauritian novel published in India was reviewed in the local Press, a couple of my friends from another school of the village came to me. They wanted to have some copies of the book to be sold among the staff which I gladly consigned to them. The next afternoon when they came back, I was, despite my bronchial problem, busy writing my second novel. They came straight to my room and after a formal chat my friend, Anand, handed a sum of hundred and twenty rupees to me for the thirty books sold at the rate of 4 rupees each. It was indeed a happy surprise to me and I said to myself— 'At least Hindi readers are showing interest in the works of local writers.' And of course I wasn't, in the least, expecting the bitter part of it until my

Slices from a Life

friend, Dharam, did let the cat out of the bag:
"Only twenty-five teachers bought the book."
"But you gave me money for thirty books."
"Because thirty books have been sold."
"I'm very dull in Arithmetic."
"Let me explain. We have four caretakers and all the four bought it."
"It makes twenty-nine."
He then took out a copy of my book from the envelope he was holding.
"If this is unsold, then how come you pay me for thirty?"
"This too is sold: The buyer of this book has bought two instead of one and let me tell you she is a Chinese girl."
I was bound to ask:
"Does she read Hindi?"
"No. Her friend knows Hindi. So she bought one for her friend and one for herself to keep it along with her collection of Mauritian writers. She has requested you to autograph this one for her both in Hindi and English."
I took the book and did as I was asked, after which Anand said to me,
"We want to tell you something unpleasant..."
He looked at Dharam who got the cue to continue the sentence.
"We are afraid that it may pain you. None of the four Hindi teachers showed any interest in your book. The eldest Guruji said it in the very beginning that novel reading is loss of time."

That was my first painful blow of being Hindi writer and it was not the last of a serial. Sharing happiness has been very easy for me but pain, as a sole treasure, I always kept it for myself. But in this two decades column, I have always been sharing with my readers from time to time a few of my agonies along with my blissful moments. So here is one more thirty-year-old pang of pain. It is again from my teaching days at Maheshwurnath Govt School. I used to have my Std VI Hindi class in the first upstairs classroom adjacent to the Social Welfare Centre. In week-ends, Hindi classes were run in the school. It did happen after a Sunday Hindi class, that is, the next day, when I entered the room to start my Std VI class, one of my girl pupils left her place, went to the windows and said to me,

"Guruji! Could you please come here?"
"Why?"
"I want to show you something."

I went to the window and cast a glance outside in the frontyard of the Social Welfare Centre. After a thorough look, I happened to see scattered pieces of a magazine. I looked at the pupil who, after acquiring my permission, went down. I saw her enter the Social Centre yard and in a couple of minutes she was back in front of the class with the collected pieces of the tattered mag in her hands. She dropped them on the table and I was able to recognize the Hindi monthly. It was the latest issue of "*Aaj Kal*", a literary magazine, published by the Government of India in New Delhi in which the first part of my serialized novel *Chowtha Prani* was published along with my photo. Holding the three torn pieces of my photo I stared at the girl and asked her,

"Who did tear it?"

She was prompt:

"I brought the magazine from my house. I thought my friends and Guruji would be very pleased to see the photo because my father showed it to everybody at home. But when I showed it to our Guruji, he snatched it and after tearing threw the pieces through the window."

After a pause she continued,

"He said to the class that we must read good literature and not trash like this. The butchered issue of *Aaj Kal* dated January 1970 had, as its content, writings of great authors like Dwivediji, Upendranath Ashk, Mahadevi Varma and Mikhael Sholokov amongst others. It was because of me that they too were branded writers of trash. Let me still not believe Nirad Chowdhry who had said, "*Envy is our national heritage*".

Slices from a Life

𝒟onation 𝒟onated

The Second World War was over and yet like several countries our island too was still undergoing days of dire straits. In those days I was a pupil in Standard III at the Maheswarnath Aided School of Triolet, where every morning we had to sing "God save the Queen" and "Britannia rules the waves". Unaware of the fact that we were praying to remain dependent of a country with 52 colonies at its disposal we enjoyed it.

In spite of the caring of our British ruler and our ration cards we were having hard time for our foodstuff provision. Only those with means were able to acquire it from the profiteers. Even potato was scarce and my mother was used to thank the huge breadfruit tree in our backyard for providing us both roti and curry. In lack of rice and flour we had to buy dried chips of potato which my mother made possible by selling milk and eggs. Split peas were the only grain available at the Chinese shop. After soaking the grain in water for a whole night my mother would grind it on the grinding stone. She would then convert it into several small balls and let them dry in the sun, after which the *adowris* were preserved in earthen pots to be used in vegetables preparations. These *adowris* were as tasty as the fresh "*Karhi Barhi*". This was done to overcome the problem of deep frying because oil was rare and very expensive. There were days when we had to opt for *Dalpitha* or *Doorimai* with coriander chutney for our dinner.

One afternoon when I was playing marble games with my friends a lorry entered our unfenced yard. The brand new looking lorry was instantly surrounded by all my friends, expressing their admiration in Bhojpuri. We were having a close look at it when a very smart looking man alighted from the lorry and inquired in creole:

"Is Monsieur Pateesing at home?"

I replied in the same,

"*Non li dan tabagie.*"

"Is it far from here?"

I indicated the tobacco shop which was at a stone's throw from us.

My father, surrounded by the elders of the neighbourhood, was reading the newspaper to them. It was under the flamboyant opposite our shop. The man in front of me who was well dressed and wearing an expensive hat on his head moved to the indicated direction. My friends and I rotated the latest model Bedford which we were seeing for the first time. Everyone was having his comments when the spick-and-span man came back to the lorry along with my father and said to the driver:

"Philippe! Give a helping hand to Sohun to bring out the rice sack."

One of the two men on the deck jumped down and the driver went up to help the other one. The heavy sack was very quickly taken out of the vehicle and laid on the head of the third person standing on the ground. When the sack of rice was being transported to our house, a friend of mine whispered to the others and then asked me with surprise in his voice:

"From where did you get it?"

I couldn't answer. Instead I asked myself:

'How could we afford to buy a whole bag of rice when everybody in the village has to implore humbly for at least one pound of rice to the shopkeeper.?'

The marble game couldn't continue. All my friends ran to tell their parents the big news. I was happy but at the same time as surprised as my friends. When I entered our house I heard my mother asking my father:

"Who was the man?"

She was referring to the man who brought the rice. My father ignored the question and said:

"There is no one attending the shop, I have to go."

My mother repeated her question and my father stepping out of the threshold said:

"I'll tell you later."

At night the question was recast and my father said that the deliverer was very rich man from Port Louis. He added, pointing the sack:

"This is a very special rice from Rangoon. It's not availale on ration cards. Too expensive."

Slices from a Life

"Then how could we afford…"

"I did not have to pay for it. It has been given to me in gratitude for service rendered."

A jargon not understood by my mother so my father simplified it:

"It's a gift. I helped him in a police case and he won. Knowing that I'll not accept any money from him he brought this present."

My mother didn't show any sign of understanding.

The day after I was at the tobacco shop when my father's bosom friend Bharat Chacha came to him a couple of hours earlier than his usual visit. After the routine questions and replies about mutual health Bharat Chacha came to the real purpose of his early visit and said:

"I'm told that you got a full bag of rice."

After the affirmative reply from my father he said:

"As you know next week my daughter is getting married. I have been able to get only 50 pounds of rice and that too with much difficulty. Your bag must be of hundred and fifty pounds."

He stopped for a while and said:

"Please sell half of it to me."

The next morning when my father was on the verge of leaving the house to proceed to the shop we got the unexpected visit of Bharat Chacha's wife.

With the help of my sister, my father divided the rice in two equal parts and gave one to Bharat Chacha. After her departure when my mother asked my father whether he was getting paid for it or it was given free my father said in Hindi:

"*Daan me daan maha daan.* (Donation donated is great donation.)"

It wasn't the first philanthropic gesture of my father that I witnessed but it was my first awareness of the reason for which I was no more the son of a well-off person.

The Source of a Trilogy

The idea of writing my trilogy 'ature *Lal Passina*' came to me through the stories I used to hear in my childhood, from my parents. Both my father and mother had heard of the struggles and sufferings of the Indian immigrants from their parents and they had also, to some extent, known and lived those painful situations. My interest in those stories was deeper than in the fairy tales. But the sparks of the idea of writing the struggling saga of the immigrants was produced in me by a few lines of a *Birha*, a painful folksong in Bhojpuri.

In those days we used to have yearly *Pooja* at the village Kalimaye. This Kalimaye ceremony was known to us as '*Baharya Pooja*' and its organiser was a devotee of Kali named Jatan Raout Gopal. A couple of weeks prior to the ceremony a few people would go around the village with *Dholak*, *Dhapli* and *Shahnai* to have it announced and collect money from the villgers. The *Pooja* was performed with fanfare in which we the children had all the fun of a festive day. The village Kalimaye was to the extreme north of Triolet in the corner of the Trou-aux-Biches road where it still is, though without the gaiety of those days. We, the children, were much eager to participate in cleaning and decorating the whole area of the Kalimaye but the opportunity given to us by the elders was not as wished.

On the day of the *Pooja* the activities started early in the morning. The surrounding of the Kalimaye was not enough commodious and for that reason devotees had to gather on the other side by the "public fountain", a more open place at that time. Jatan Gopal, with bare chest in knee-up *dhoti* and large *Tika* on his forehead and all over his naked part looked very imposing. There were several glandular swellings on his brown body of which we, the children, were very amazed. Even his moustache was very funny and attractive at the same time. During the *Pooja*, when he took boiling milk from the earthen cauldron and sprinkle it on his bare chest I got terribly alarmed. After a few other rituals his whole body, possessed by the deity, started shaking and with a rattan rod in his hand he went on round the altar. Brandishing the rod with tremendous speed and outcrying the name of Kali when he passed by us we had to step back in fear.

In the last part of the *Pooja* the women went near the Kali altar to offer '*Khir Poori*' to the goddess and to share *sindoor*. The last ritual of the *Baharya Pooja* was the sacrifice for which goats were garlanded and made ready for the purpose. This was the only part of the *pooja* scenes which after having seen it once I never saw it again. The man with the sabre was Laikwa of whom it was said that he had been conferred upon him the boon of the deity for the use of his sabre to sacrifice the goats. When I saw him spotting his sabre, with the vermillion *sindoor*, on the first occasion I was really thrilled. There were five goats on that day for the sacrifice, all of them garlanded with marigold garlands. When the long sabre of Laikwa rose to strike with the rays of the midday sun I was taken by terror. I wanted to run away from there but before my steps could obey my mind, the sabre of the performer had already reached the neck of the black goat. The exploding fountain of blood made me feel giddy and I had to leave the place. I, of course, attended all the *Baharya Poojas* after that but every time I left the place at the very moment when the man with the sabre had to come in action.

After the *pooja* at the Kalimaye devotees had to attend another custom at Jatan's place and that was for the sacrificial *prasad*. The remaining half day and almost the whole night were for drinking, eating and rejoicing. As sacrificial meat was not accepted in our family I was forbidden to participate in the post *pooja* merriment and yet I used to be present there for the songs and dances. My parents hadn't to worry about it because in those days I happened to be a vegetarian despite all the convincing tactics of my nurse Madame Lebon who wanted me to have at least accepted egg because of my frail body.

I was very fond of listening to the Birhas that were sung on that occasion by those ordinary people. They carried in them both a story and a tit for tat presence of mind on the part of the singers. The songs when reached to climax were accompanied by fast beats of *dholak* and *dhapli*. There were also moments when even listeners started dancing. There was one man, with half baldness, among those singers of

Birha from Mon Choisy known to us by his nickname of Pompier Ahee. His one hand holding a wine bottle and with the other hand on his ear he was the most cheered Birha singer, non-pareil.

He was as drunk as always on that specific day when women cooking the sacrificial meat at Jatan's place were also busy in their usual gossip. The Birha singers had to raise their voice to a higher pitch in order to overcome that of the women. Despite his drunkenness Pompier was able to maintain the depth of his voice and his presence of mind in replying his contestant. We were all enjoying the climax when someone came to tell Pompier that he was being waited for the meal. This request was repeated for two more times within fifteen minutes but Pompier paid no heed to it. He went on singing non-stop.

It was believed that pompier was expert in composing instantly his lines and nobody could have doubted it. The way he was in the habit of giving the tit for tat, the contestant singer was an evident in itself. Everybody was thrilled by his wit and humour and of course I was one of them. But then there were those lines of his that, though without any great impact of others, had disturbed me immensely. It was an invitation to contemplate on the destiny of man. Replying to one of his singer friends he had rendered those lines in a painful voice. Without providing the exact lines of the song I am giving here the gist of it:

"O Lord of the sugar estate! Why are you exhausting yourself now? Hold on your whip. Stop it. My back is full of slashing marks. There is no place left on it for any print. What's the use of tiring yourself by slashing in vain?"

The stories that were told to me by my mother and father and which I had to live them mentally became more acidic and made me more restless. And those very lines of Pompier Aheer, though years later, were rotating in my mind when I had to start my trilogy '*Lal Passina*'. The only scene, out of so many of the *Baharya Poojas* of my village, that is still so lucid in my mind is that explosive Birha. Now whenever I come to think of that sad song of the labourers it seems to me as though the voice of Pompier Aheer was perhaps the resonance of the pain of the first Indian labourers of this country. Unrecorded in history books and yet echoing from every pyramid of rocks in our cane fields.

Slices from a Life

Month Without Pay Day

Speaking of the pang of hunger, the one speaking in Hindi will express it— "*Mere pet me choohe kood rahe hein*", that is "Mice are somersaulting in my stomach". In creole it is expressed in a different tone when it is said that "*mo vente pe sente—God save the Queen*". But the real pang of hunger remains most of the time unexpressed. Those who have known it have preferred not to share it with others. And what if after having gone to every nook and corner for a morsel of bread you happen to come to someone who offers you a brick in the form and name of bread. And what if believing it to be a real one you immediately take it to your mouth and then hear the benefactor bursting into laughter.

There are, of course, people who can go to the extent of such a waggery. Those were the days of dire straits and I had to carry in me my hunger as well as that of my parents. But it was the echo of "No Vacancy" that gave me a bigger pang. After a long endeavour I had got the job of a receiver in the Rose Hill Bus Service which I had to lose it because I issued a ten cent lesser ticket to a beggar. Going round the village with a huge basket of vegetables on my head did not help much. Looking for a job was the most painful task.

One morning, I was on the road when a short-statured man known to me as Parashwa, talking to an obese person near the Kalimaye, stopped me and said:

"I'm told that you are wandering unsucessfully for a job! You should have come to me..."

"Could you help me getting a job?" I asked him.

"Of course, I can. Immediately, if you want."

He then looked at the obese man and asked him:

"What do you say Dhansam *Bhaye*! We give him the job?"

The man addressed as Dhansam, with his effeminate voice, replied in the same serious tone.

"Oh, yes! He is an intelligent boy, he can do it."

The corrugated tin building opposite us in which my father used to have his second tobacco shop has its second part occupied a few days back by Habib, the barber. The room was vacated by him because of a quarrel provoked by a discussion on Raj Kapoor and Dilip Dumar with the youngsters of the locality. With his hand on my shoulder Parashwa took me to the closed barber's shop and asked the owner, who was tearing off the cinema posters from the wall, to bring him the key. Chingroo brought the key and the room was opened. As we went inside, Parashwa in his serious voice said:

"Dhansam *Bhaiya* and I are going to open a branch office of our union. We are giving you the responsibility of this office. Within a week a typist will join you. We are also arranging for a phone. But are you sure to be able to tackle?"

"If you initiate me just once I am sure to manage?"

"First of all we need a table and a chair. It will take a few days before the complete set of furniture reaches here. For the meantime you have to bring a table and a chair from your place. The work has to start as from today. Today being Tuesday and the first day of the month it is an auspicious day."

I ran to my house to inform my sister "*Tifi*" of the good news. She let me take the small table and an old chair. I brought the brown table first and then the chair to Chingroo's building. Parashwa told me that they would be giving me a hundred rupees to start with. He added:

"It will be increased after a couple of months. Do you agree?"

I was not so foolish to say no. I had wandered for months for a job of much lesser. I couldn't have thought of hundred rupees. I was very happy to have acquired more than desired. This time it was Dhansam who told me:

"As from tomorrow you will have the stationery".

It was the turn of Parashwa to go on explaining to me the work to be done. After half an hour when both were leaving the place I heard behind them a combined laughter.

I had started weaving and cherishing a dream thinking that when God gives it comes from the blue. Till yesterday, I was knocking every door to obtain a job and today unexpectedly it has come to me by itself. Thing for which I was looking places far away was just by my house. A few minutes later, it was Carrim Mamoo who came to me and in a teasing tone said:

Slices from a Life

"Salam *Sahib*! This is a very good job."

"It is due to the kindness of Parashwa and Dhansam *Bhaiya*.

"You are a fool despite your learning. How could it be that the son of Patee *Bahnoyi* is such a stupid! You have been made a fool by Parashwa and Dhansamwa. This is not an office."

I was stupefied.

"But Mamoo, this room has been rented..."

"This room has been rented by Parashwa to have his tobacco leaves stored in for drying".

It was as though I was tightly holding the stone bread in my hands. With pain inside me I asked myself:

"What did Parashwa and Dhansamwa get by making fun of me?"

Well! Whatever the pleasure they derived from it, it remained theirs. And yet I did get something out of it. It was the same Parashwa who years later had to come to me, when his son, who was taught by me free of cost, had succeeded in becoming a Hindi teacher. On that day, I just said to him:

"This is going to be a long life for him. Not for minutes only."

Fête Cabas and My First Earning

My readers are aware of the fact that before I started working as a teacher, that is from the age of fourteen to eighteen, I had to go for several types of work. But there was an unusual sort of work I happened to do which I always hesitated to speak of. Today I am bound to accept that the strange job was in a way apprenticeship of my writing. It is known to all of us that everyone is a poet in his youth and his lover his first reader of his poems. It started the other way with me. I started writing letters to my countrymen working far away from their country. My French and English were both as bad as they are today. The irony was that there was hardly one or two among those, whom I used to write, who were able to read those letters.

It happened in the early 1950's, that is when I started the job. I was 12 years old. Some twenty persons from my neighbourhood had joined the Pioneer Corps and serving in Egypt. A few of them were married. It was Rabia who came to me first with the letter of her husband Moustouf. It was the first letter of Moustouf from Egypt. Rabia was slim, very good-looking who always talked in a very cultured way though she had never been to school. Her marriage had hardly completed its two years when her husband got recruited in the Pioneer Corps of Her Majesty's Service. Jawahar and I were the only two students in the vicinity attending college in Port Louis. I used to call Rabia *Bhabhi*, meaning sister-in-law but when my mother, after explaining me the village customary relationship with Moustouf's family, asked me to call her *Didi*, that is sister, I had to accept. From that very day Rabia was my *Didi*. After handing me the letter she said:

"You alone can read the letter and tell how is your brother-in-law doing there."

I opened the letter and started going through it. Because of the bad handwriting it wasn't an easy task. The letter was

Slices from a Life

written in a melange of French and Creole. As Moustouf couldn't read and write it was understood that the letter was written by one of his Mauritian friends. After reading a few lines I had to stop and give Rabia *Didi* a rendering in Bhojpuri with a mix of Creole words. I looked at her while explaining. The content of the letter was tangible proof that Moustouf was happy there but I couldn't understand why Rabia started shedding tears.

The next day she came back with a writing sheet and an envelope. I told her that reading the letter and explaining it to her was all right but writing to her husband on her behalf was a hard nut to crack. She insisted and I had to submit to her sweet words but when I asked her what to write she very innocently said:

"You write whatever you feel good."

So her first letter. I wrote it, without her saying anything, in my own words. She was very pleased when I read the letter to her with rendering in Bhojpuri. Once started she continued coming to me after every fortnight or so to have her letters read and written and with time she expressed her thoughts and feeling in Bhojpuri and I wrote them in French.

It was the turn of Ramdeo's wife Dularia, my sister Amawtee, the mother of Koodoos and Inoos, the widow Pagalia Bhowjee, Suzanne, Chengna's mistress and others to follow suit. I was unwillingly made a licensed letter writer of some twenty wives, mothers and sisters. Inoos's mother would go on crying with every letter read and written. Whenever, after reading her letters, I said that her two sons Koodoos and Inoos were in good health and enjoying life there she wouldn't believe it easily and repeat asking:

"*Babooa*, are you telling me the truth?"

And when I emphasized on my words she kissed me on both my cheeks and said:

"You are my sweetest little brother-in-law."

The husband of Dularia was a complete stranger to the written words. The person who wrote his letters in Egypt seemed to be a well read person in a good official rank. His French was very good and even the few lines in English in almost all the letters addressed to Dularia were very neat. My letters also carried a few lines in English. Chengna's wife requested me to write her letters in English because the letters were read there by a British friend of Chengna. She always came to me with letters in hiding because her relation with Chengna wasn't approved by the parents of her man.

The wives of the Pioneers serving in the British army in Egypt, Italy and elsewhere were allocated a monthly pension by the Government. This pension was known in the public as "fête cabas" because the Pioneers' wives on that great day were dressed up to the nines to go to the pension office. It was indeed a festival of the lady's handbag. Bhai Hamja who had the best car around used to do the monthly trip from Triolet to Pamplemousses or sometime to Port Louis pension office and back with Rabia *Didi* and her four friends. If the "fête cabas" happened to be a great day for the parents and families of the pioneers it wasn't less important to me. It meant that I was able to make an earning with my pen. It was again Rabia who started it and was followed after by all others whose letters I read and wrote. On the first occasion, despite my refusal, Rabia gave one rupee and as from the third month two rupees on every "fête cabas" and the same was done by the others. My mother wasn't agreeable to any payment who said to them that all services cannot be paid by money but then it was a question of majority so they won.

Thus the "fête cabas" became my pay day for almost five years and I earned thirty to forty rupees per month which meant a lot in those days. The first income of my pen. A process to give meaning to the feelings of others through my words which continues today, though in a different way. My mother didn't take a single cent out of that income and the next day of every "fete cabas" I ran to Nalanda and the Libraire Seneque in Port Louis to afford myself one month's reading.

Punishment Without Tears

The area where is situated the Trou-aux-Biches Village Hotel was at that time an open coconut orchard. On the other side of the road was forest of casuarina trees in the midst of which there were tall coconut trees older than my father. In between there was a marsh with white earth and around it, because of the water of the marsh, was the most green plains of the area—the playground of the youngsters of Triolet North. It was a time when children were not able to afford for a real soccer ball and instead of it were used to collect old and tattered rugs and gave it the form of a football. Our other alternative was a big round grapefruit which was dehardened by us and with which we played for hours. I was then of eleven or twelve. My father was working as overseer of the property of Dr Jhuboo, which started from the border of Mont Choisy Estate to end at the beginning of Pointe-aux-Piments. There were three overseers to look after the whole property amongst which my father was chief. He was the last of the three to join for the job which he got because of his age. It was again because of his age that he was given the seniority by Dr Jhuboo. He was also the most respected one. It was my father's long-time-after employment that enabled us to forget days of dire straits.

We, the children of the locality, hardly half-mile away from Dr Jhuboo's estate were in the habit of crossing the filao and coconut trees to reach the sesside. In the days of school vacation we spent our whole day swimming and fishing for which most of us were punished on returning home. I too would forget the thrashing I got from my mother to run again next day to our so cherished spot. There were also days when carrying the lunch of my father I went on wandering on the beach. My father was never found on a specific place. Sometimes I was on the Mont Choisy border where people were cutting down filao trees and dressing and branches very neatly in small pyramid form for the producing of coals. On other occasions I would find my father among the three boys of my age who were grazing the cattle by the Pointe-aux-Piments side. The incident I am going to relate here is of a blazing afternoon. On that day one of the overseers, Dhanwa, was away and my father had to make a round of the whole orchard in the Pointe-aux-Piments area where stealing of coconut was aften reported.

After leaving my father's lunch basket in the custody of Hareea, the herdboy, I went straight to the seaside where my friends were already having their swim in the crystal clear water of the waveless sea. Those were unrestrained moments when we used to play and enjoy in the water on the sand and in the orchard in such a self-willed way as though the whole place belonged to us and only us. Those were days when the feeling of being stranger in our own land never came to our minds. In the August heat the water of the sea was providing such a coolness to the body that despite the proceeding of some of our friends to Mont Choisy a few of us remained in the cool water of Trou-aux-Biches. I was with Aneeroodwa. And Mohna and Talebwa were at a small distance away in deeper sea. We were competing with each other but as we two were not as good swimmers as Mohna and Talebwa, we were the first to get tired and came out of the water to lie dishevelled on the sand. We watched our two friends swimming in the direction of Mont Choisy.

Later, when after putting on our clothes we came under the coconut trees we saw two men drinking coconut milk. A whole bunch of big ones was lying near them. It did not take us much time to know that they had made capital out of the absence of the overseers. Both looked at us, at our tiredness and our interest in the lying coconuts and after exchanging glances one of them asked us:

"Would you like to drink?"

Before I could say yes, Aneeroodwa nodded. The tallest of the two men threw his drained coco in the direction of the sea and took hold of the knife from his friend. He cut the upper parts of two coconuts and handed them to us. They were big enough and known to us as Coco Ceylan, containing more than one litre of sweet water. We were so thirsty that we took them to our mouths in such a haste that we dropped on our chests and on the ground almost the same quantity of water that went into our stomach. Before we left one of them gave us two more coconuts and said:

Slices from a Life

"Get lost before the watchman sees you."

It was heavy and like Aneeroodwa, I also put it under my armpit and still holding it with my right hand took the road to home. We were not aware of the exact time yet because of the sun's position we guessed it to be around four. In the still blazing sun with the heavy enough gift under our arms we have just entered the Shivala enclave when a man coming from behind on a bicycle stopped us. He took hold of Aneeroodwa'a arm and rebuking very sharply said:

"You both have to accompany me to the police station!"

I knew the man. He was the second overseer of Dr Jhuboo's estate. I even knew his name but he did not know me. He was called Pitka. He continued on his overtone:

"You bastards! You have stolen coconuts from the orchard. I'll take you first to the boss. You both follow me."

I was of course very afraid but Aneeroodwa's state was worse. We had no alternative but to follow Pitka back to the seaside where Dr Jhuboo had his bungalow. When we arrived there Dr Jhuboo was sitting in front of his bungalow under the "Badamier" and grilling maize on embers. Putting both of us in front of him, Pitka said:

"They were running away after stealing coconuts."

Dr Jhuboo did not look at us immediately. He changed sides of the two half grilled maize on the charcoal and then turned to us with reprimanding voice:

"You rogues! Do these coconut trees belong to your fathers?"

We remained silent. Our silence made him more angry.

We were struck with fear and remained dumb. Dr Jhuboo ordered Pitka:

"Take these two rascals and hand them over to the police."

Aneeroodwa started crying. I automatically joined my hands and stood wordless. Dr Jhuboo fixed his eyes on us— eyes which were not at all cruel. Burning smell came out of the maize. He at once took them out of the embers, looked at us again and then said to the overseer:

"You will find money inside. Take a rupee and bring me some butter and salt from the shop. In the meantime I will be watching these scoundrels."

A few minutes after the departure of Pitka, Dr Jhuboo looked at us and asked:

"Who is the elder of you two?"

Aneeroodwa said he was.

"How is it then that you are dwarfish? All right... You go there and bring me the billhook."

When Aneeroodwa went for the billhook, Dr Jhuboo asked me:

"You look as though you belong to a respected family and yet you are a thief. What is the name of your father?"

I was already very much fear-stricken. The question frightened me more because I knew that if my father came to know of this I shall be in big trouble. My father, in his anger, will never believe of my innocence.

In a low voice, I gave a wrong name. Aneeroodwa was back with the billhook. The doctor ordered to cut the two coconuts atop. My friend very obediently did what he was asked to do. The doctor said:

"I'll let one of you go but on one condition. Whoever of you will be the first to climb that coconut tree in front of us and come down with a coconut will be free to go. Ok! Go on!"

But when we both did not move a single step he asked:

"So you prefer going to the police?"

Aneeroodwa in trembling voice said:

"No one of us can climb a tree."

After observing us for a few seconds he said:

"Listen! It will take some five to seven minutes for Pitka to come back. He will never let you go. But if you really want to save yourself from being taken to the police, you do one thing..."

He paused and then very authoritatively said:

"Take these two opened coconuts in your hands and if each of you happened to drink a whole one without dropping a single drop, I'll let you go. If you cannot I will entrust you to the watchman."

Aneeroodwa was the first to take the coco to his mouth. I also hurried to do it but I had hardly put it to my mouth and let my forehead up when some coconut water ran through my cheeks to my shirt. The doctor warned me:

"Mind you of another drop. You will not leave this place."

I had not drunk half of the content when I started suffocating. The doctor scolded me:

"You have only one minute."

I started drinking again. Aneeroodwa went on drinking non-stop. I had to break once again and Dr Jhuboo warned

Slices from a Life

me. At last we both were able to finish the allotted job and the doctor, addressing us with a big abusing word, said:

"And now before Pitka comes, you try to run as fast as possible."

Hardly heard we ran from there with all might and main despite one full litre of water in the belly.

Made in England

The little doll my sister loved so much looked very much like a European blonde. My sister always had it dressed in the way of the English lady whose photo appeared on the tin cover of the biscuit box in which my sister kept her sewing material. The doll was indeed very beautiful and for that reason I was also very fond of it. But my father, though he bought it himself, didn't like it much because as my mother said, it was made in Japan. I was already aware of the fact that products from Japan were said to be inferior to those coming from England and France and were not considered as long-lasting.

Those were the days when we happened to sing "God saves the Queen" and "Britannia rules the waves" in the schools. I was having the last days of my incomplete schooling at the Neo College in Port-Louis. I didn't have the least notion at that time that I'll have to give up my studies in the mid term of form two. In spite of the dire straits of those days my mother fought tooth and nail to have my education continued. I stayed at my elder sister's place in Port-Louis the whole week and came home on weekends. This was done to save my parents from the burden of the everyday bus fare. But there was also the monthly fee of the college. When it became overdue I had no alternative but saying farewell to college. The story being told here goes back to the days when I was still a dull and timid student of the Neo College.

The rainy season had started. Having spent the two days of the weekend among my village friends on Monday morning I was packing my school bag when my father came to me. He tended a ten-rupee note to me and said:

"Buy an umbrella for me."

He then told me of a couple of shops in the town where I could get a good one and he said to me more than once:

"Do not bring me an umbrella made in Japan. You see to it that it is "Made in England".

I was given sixty cents for both-way bus fare and one

rupee as pocket money for the whole week. On some rare occasions, when my mummy did afford to have a little saving by selling eggs or the monthly payment by the milkman I was given two rupees instead of one rupee sixty cents but it only happened once in a blue moon. Having ten rupees in my pocket along with the one rupee sixty cents given to me by my mother I was much richer than my two co-travellers Adam and Jawahur. My mother also was conscious of the fact so she repeated her advice:

"Beware of pickpockets when you get out of the bus and do not forget to have the money in your sister's custody until you go for the shopping."

Abiding by the advice of my mother, I handed the money to my sister and told her that I'll take it back on Friday morning. Days in Port-Louis have been my longest days. Friday seemed far away to me so on Wednesday morning I took back the money from my sister saying that as I was getting an early release from college I'll be able to buy the umbrella. An idea that came to me the day before pushed me to go for the purchase of the umbrella much earlier. The strange idea came to me while I was thinking of a second advice given to me by my father. I was about to buy the British umbrella in spite of its being more expensive than the Japanese. I was discussing the matter with a friend at the college on Tuesday when I came to know that he bought an umbrella last week for seven rupees. Everyone at the college was talking about the new release at the "*Cinema-des-familes*". It was a new adventure of "*Zorro*". There were thrilling posters of the film in every nook and corner. I wanted to see the film at all costs. When a couple of friends and I came to know of the matinee show on Thursday we decided to take the risk to attend. My friends were used to such risk but for me it was the first.

I had my sleep very late on Tuesday night because of the longing. I remained thinking of acquiring an umbrella like my friend in seven rupees. With the remaining three rupees I could easily have my ticket for the matinee show and could also buy the collection of "*Grimm's Fairy Tales*" from Librairie Seneque which I was so yearning for.

Wednesday afternoon after leaving the college I went to the Royal Road before going to my sister's place at Maupin Street. After beating the air from one shop to another I, at last, entered a Chinese shop where I found two types of black umbrellas. Both had bamboo handles as wished by my father. I examined both of them. One was from England and the other from Japan. The price of the 'Made in England' was nine rupees and that of the Japan at seven rupees fifty cents. I re-examined the two mades and didn't find any apparent difference. After a slight bargain the shopkeeper accepted to give me the "Made in Japan" for seven rupees. I purchased it and with three rupees in my pocket returned to my sister's place.

The next morning when my sister and my brother-in-law were busy in the kitchen, I opened the umbrella and looked at the spot where it was written "Made in Japan". I had seen my sister cleaning stains from clothes on several occasions, with the special solutions. Pretending to clean a stain from my school bag I started removing the imprint of "Made in Japan" from the umbrella. After continuous rub I succeeded in my dishonest manoeuvre. I was ashamed of cheating my father and also afraid of his anger in case my guilt was discovered. But the desire for the book of stories and the film was stronger.

I bought the book of *Grimm's Fairy Tales* on Thursday morning for two rupees. At lunch time my friends and I managed to escape from college. We went to "Luxor Hotel" where I spent forty cents out of the remaining rupee on lunch consisting of bread-butter, gateaux pimentos and coca-cola. It was a feast. At quarter to one in the afternoon we were in the cinema hall. After paying thirty cents for the ticket I still had another thirty cents left in my pocket. We enjoyed the film, clamouring throughout.

At night I went on thinking about ways and means to save my- self from the wrath of my father if my mischief was caught. I came to the only conclusion. I'll tell him that it was the only type of umbrella available and I paid eight rupees for it. He couldn't be angry for spending two rupees on the book. Next evening I was back home. As usual I was happy to be among my friends for the weekend and going to the beaches with them but at the same time I was scared of my misdeed. When I handed the umbrella to my father I was instantly reminded of my last punishment. After opening it he asked:

"How much you paid?"

Slices from a Life

I was expecting the question so the answer came instantly:

"Eight rupees."

"And what about the remaining two rupees?"

Without saying anything I just put the book of fairy tales in front of him. He said nothing and went to read the newspaper to his friend waiting under the flamboyant tree. I got a great relief. My crime wasn't detected. But I was wrong. The next morning my mother talked to me in the kitchen:

"You should never do it again."

"What?"

"You thought that by removing the Japanese name from the umbrella you could have fooled your father. Look, my son, your father has been teaching and advising hundreds of people in this village. It isn't so easy to cheat him."

And I was really ashamed of my deed.

It was some twenty years later that my father reminded me of the instance when the Japanese market was gaining momentum and proving its superiority upon European products. It was raining heavily outside. After opening the old tattered umbrella in his hand he said:

"The same Japan that was collapsed and shattered in the big war is today ruling the waves."

The Taste of the Roasted Hare

It was the beginning of dire straits in the family and my father was bound to work as *Sirdar* in Dr Jhubboo's estate. But as the meagre salary was inadequate to make the two ends meet, my mother had to continue with the cattle breeding. It was the last year of my primary schooling and I had to help my mother to provide fodder for the two cows and a few goats. It was also the days when my health had started deteriorating and I had to be in transit between home and the Civil Hospital in Port-Louis. The Sir Seewoosagur Ramgoolam National Hospital was not yet thought of its raison d'être. When one of our cows became sterile and the other was unable to stand on her feet our income from cattle breeding was suddenly brought to an end.

The small farmers of Triolet, at that period, had to hire land from Dr Jhubboo for the cultivation of vegetables and tobacco. My father too hired an acre of land at that specific area of Trou-aux-Biches and we started getting rid of the dense bushes and unnecessary trees all around. As my father was very much taken up with his work it was up to my sister and me to help my mother in the deforesting. We had to employ a couple of labourers on temporary basis to prepare the land for planting, specially when we had to provide coal from the fallen trees. During the first plantation we employed Ramdewa, one in our neighbourhood, on regular basis. He was weekly paid out of the money my mother used to get by selling hens and eggs. Even that income wasn't sufficient so later on my mother had to borrow two hundred rupees from Aunty Harbasseea by mortgaging her jewellery.

From my very childhood I liked the smell of the earth and for that reason I enjoyed working in the field. My mother didn't like my joining her and working in the scorching sun and rain because of my ill health. On school days I attended the field only on weekends but during the vacation I went to give a helping hand almost everyday. As the sea was at a stone's throw I spent half the day with my friends by the seaside and the other half in the plantation. Our acre of land my father got it a bit cheaper because part of the plot was covered with basalt. There was a sandalwood tree in the midst and a well whose water we used for watering. The first well that Ramdewa dug was useless because of its salty water.

Our vegetables field was not too far from the marshy land where today the Trou-aux-Biches Hotel has its golf pitch. I used to watch our field getting its verdant colour with eagerness. The brinjal plants were the first to bear flowers and much later the tomato as they were replanted a month later. I was anxiously waiting for the vegetables to come and my mother would say to me.

I haven't known any woman as laborious as my mother. After her whole day work in the plantation she got busy collecting fodder for the cattle. Ramdewa was some four to five years my elder. He too was of the opinion that my mother despite her slim and weak-looking body was very courageous and never looked tired. When in his mood Ramdewa was indeed a hard worker but when out of mood he would avoid being sighted by my mother and start targetting at birds with his pellet bows made out of rubber band. Among the few filao and coconut trees in the field there was a special type of bird said to be "Collier de Mer". When I first heard the bird chirping I looked around me to find out who was whistling. Ramdewa who was behind me smiled at my surprise and said:

"You are thinking that someone around is whistling? Oh no! Look at the tree; it's the "Collier de Mer".

And really when I looked at the filao tree to my great amazement I saw one of the couple of birds singing with tail up, and it was as though a man was whistling.

In matter of days and weeks the plants started bearing brinjal and tomato. I happened to go to the big rock near the sandalwood tree to admire the beauty of our vegetables garden. From within the green leaves, violet brinjals were peeping at me and from here and there couples of half-red tomatoes swinging in the green bush. Since a few days a few hares were causing havoc to the plantation and mother was much disturbed. It was the beginning of winter and because of dense cloud in the sky the sun hadn't appeared yet as usual; it wasn't difficult to guess that mid-day wasn't too far. Ramdewa was always waiting for the tolling of the church bell in order to go to the sandalwood tree with his lunch bag.

The coals obtained out of the woods during the deforesting were put in gunny bags and sold but there were still tiny pieces of coals scattered here and there on the sandy soil. I saw my mother picking up some pieces of coal and dry branches of filao and producing embers in front of the small thatched hut. I thought that she was doing so because of the pertaining cold but I was wrong. During the free time my father had sowed seeds of garlic, spring onions and coriander in three separate beds by the well not in use. Every afternoon back from his work he himself watered the plants. I saw my mother very precautiously uprooting one plant from each bed and then plucking two brinjals of her choice. In the meantime the embers were in full blaze. My mother picked up a stick from the ground and after making a few holes in the two brinjals she thrust pieces of garlic inside and put them on the embers. She asked me to bring to her a couple of ripe tomatoes which I did immediately to help my mother at preparing the "*Baigan bharta*", that is the chutney of brinjal. As the grilling proceeded, the air became imbibed with the aroma of the roasted brinjals. As I was very fond of *Baigan's* chutney I got hungry before time. Mother took out the food bowl from the bag and opened it. She prepared the "*Baigan harta*" in the cover of the bowl.

The church bell started its ding-dong and when Ramdewa after taking hold of his food bag wanted to rush to his lunch spot my mother stopped him and asked him to join us. The three of us sat by the fire and the meal we had was so luscious that cannot be easily forgotten. Never again I had that taste of *Baigan's* chutney in my life. Even today I'm reminded of it whenever *Baigan's bharta* is prepared at home.

There was another unforgettable event that took place on that day. As mentioned before a group of hares were ravaging our plantation. My mother had sowed some beans in between the brinjal and tomato plants which were grazed by the hares overnight. Three days earlier Ramdewa had set up traps for them at different parts of the field but not a single one was entrapped. In the afternoon when Ramdewa was filling brinjals in a gunny bag by sprinkling water for better pressing I was standing by him. The pressing was producing a sound like *quink-quink* that I liked to listen.

My mother had left after plucking some green tomatoes

on the other side of the basalt. It was the first harvest and in order to take them home to ripen I took an empty bag and went to collect them on the side of Uncle Janki's land. I had to cross the stone parapet to reach the place where the tomatoes were left. Suddenly I had to stop because I heard a strange noise. I looked in the direction of the parapet from where the painful noise was coming. I saw a hare caught in the trap set by Ramdewa struggling to get free. I was happy at the first instant on the success of Ramdewa but then witnessing the painful situation of the hare my joy faded. The hare went on struggling and moaning.

In the morning when we were on our way to the field Ramdewa had told me that if not today then tomorrow he was going to have at least one hare trapped. To a question of his I replied that I had never tasted hare meat and he promised me to make me taste roasted hare. In those days I was a vegetarian, a fact I didn't reveal to Ramdewa. I was looking at the listless hare due to pain. I was scared to go nearer. I looked at the eastern direction where Ramdewa was busy tuning a film tune and filling the brinjals. I took courage and went nearer to the suffering animal. When it saw me coming closer its struggling increased. I stood brooding as to what to do/what not to do. If I happen to shout and tell Ramdewa of the big catch he would come running with joy. I picked up a stick that was lying at my feet and tried to press the wire entangling the hare's foot. The exercise wasn't an easy one. I tried several times and at last succeeded in loosening the noose.

Without losing a second the hare ran away with all speed.

The Days of Ajanta Arts

Those were my days of TV plays on the MBCTV. It was in 1966-67 when no pre-recording was done. Artists had to present their items in black and white and in live in the "*Chand Tare*" slot. I was writing, directing and playing the main roles of my TV plays under the banner of Ajanta Arts of Triolet. I was a school teacher at that time, days when no primary school teacher could afford to have a car. My group, comprising of a dozen artists for every put-up, had the privilege of being transported to the MBC studio by generous persons like Deochand Nundlall of the T.B.S. and Drona Seeku of the Mauritius Bakers. It was much later that the MBC provided transport to the performers. My first was entitled "*Nowlakha Haar*" which, because of its great demand, was broadcast live on three occasions with different casts. Among some forty plays presented by the Ajanta Arts and produced by the MBCTV, the following were hits: "*Billi Ko Dafna Do*", "*Raksha Bandhan*", "*Khooni Ab Bhi Daw Raha*" and "*Panchi Jahan Dam Lete Hein*", just to mention a few, to offer a feeling of nostalgia of the glorious past to our fans of that period. Most of my actors and actresses later worked in my stage productions as very accomplished artists, in full length plays such as "*Goonga Itihas*", "*Nowshera Ka Yatri*", "*Urmilla*" and other plays. This reminiscence, appearing in *Mot a Mot* column, took place during the production of "*Pooja ke Phool*" when our local TV station was one year old. The creative days when Yacoob Bahemia was producer and promoter of Arts and Culture at Forest Side. For the live performance of "*Pooja Ke Phool*", some of our artists had to travel by bus with night stay arrangements at their relatives'. Along with the three remaining artists, including Pandit Vishnu Sharma, I left Triolet at about 6.00 in the afternoon with Deochand Nundlall in his Toyota. The live telecast was scheduled for 7.30 p.m. We did have two previous rehearsals on the already mounted set, as needed by me, in the presence of the producer, the light designer, the sound recordist and other technicians. So I was very sure of my actors. It was my only no-heroine play. My friend Nundlall, being very precautious, was a slow driver. On our way to the MBC, I had to request him from time to time to be a bit faster so that we might reach the studio on time. Reassuring us, he said very confidently, "Don't worry, we will not be late". But I continued requesting at every slow down, "The character of the opening scene, the Pundit, is with us, let's move faster."

My eyes were moving to and fro now on the clock of the car and then on the speedometer. After crossing Port Louis when the speed increased to forty miles per hour, I let my uneasiness decrease. I was conscious of the make-up problem. On some occasions when the makeup person did not turn up I had to do it myself for the whole cast for which I had to carry a make-up kit with me all the time. I wished that at least today the makeup man would make it a must, otherwise we would not be ready for the set in time. The irony wants it that whenever someone is late, hindrances come to add to it. From Beau Bassin to Rose Hill, we were not given clear line to overtake and were bound to follow two lazy heavy weight trucks. We had to wait our arrival at Belle Rose in order to gradually increase the speed of our brand new car from 20 to 60 km per hour. I started worrying for the make-up and silently recited all the prayers I had missed during the last days to reach MBC by quarter to seven to avoid the last hour tension.

We were reaching our destination when the least expected came to happen. We were in the Mosque area of Phoenix when unexpectedly a child crossed the road from behind a bus. Despite an instant full brake by the driver, the worse could not be avoided and the car hit the boy. Fortunately enough the accident occurred when the car was on the verge of stopping fully. We all stepped out from the car and went to the boy. The latter was slightly bumped at his knee. I took hold of his leg and thanked God for not finding any scratch or bleeding. In the meantime people had surrounded us with hostile address. Their main target was the driver. In spite of assuring them that the child was safe with no injury, the vociferation reached a crescendo of anger. Deochand was, no doubt, the most afraid of us all. In the light of the pole-bulb overhead I let my eyes roam over the facial aggressive expressions of the mob and looking at the oldest one I said:

"The boy came all of a sudden from the rear side of a bus".

My excuse was rejected by the angry voice of a youngster:

"You were at excess speed F. . . .ou *mama*."

I tried to explain further:

"See! There is no wound at all."

"Are you a doctor? There might be inner injuries."

From the mid of the brouhaha a man with a white *topee* on his head came forward and started looking at me—

"Are you not the TV..."

I immediately responded:

"Yes I am. We are proceeding to the MBC for our tonight's programme."

It seemed that nobody was interested in any explanation. The man with the white prayer cap went to the child and asked him:

"Can you walk? Have you any pain?"

The still stunned boy replied in a slow voice:

"Yes I can walk."

"What about pain?"

"No pain."

The man with the white *topee* talked to the aggressive crowd after which he assured me. In the meantime my friend Nundlall fished out his visiting card from his pocket and handing it to our benefactor said:

"If in case there is any serious injury, please give me a ring."

Someone from the mid of the crowd came closer to Nundlall and expressed with surprise:

"But you are our patron. No problem, I'll look after."

We were then allowed to leave the hot spot. On the way Nundlall told us that the person who addressed him was a member of the company who was the builder of bodies of his buses. It started showering. When we arrived at the MBCTV everyone at the studio was looking disappointed. Only seven minutes left. The producer was already looking for some items to fill the gap and an anchor person was standing by for the second camera to announce the other programme instead of "*Puja ke Phool.*" I lost no second to go straight in front of the producer who after seeing me had a feeling of relief. He announced: "Only six minutes."

And gave last instructions to the unit.

"Stand by. Artists, take position. Hurry up for voice test,

Slices from a Life

light adjustment."

Cameraman was asked to be ready for the red light. At the very right time the live broadcast of "*Puja ke Phool*" started and went to its viewers. It was the days of Ajanta Arts in 1966-1967, the golden age of local creative productions, the first steps towards the making of serials, 35 years back, yet to be realized.

The Expensive Coin

    The barber's name, who used to come to our place on every second day to shave my father, was Mamade Issac. He lived at Neuvième Mile, not very far way from ours. Our house was of thatched roof and it was in its extreme room facing the main road that I had my sleeping bed. My father's bed also was in the same room beside my "collègien"—the single iron bed. Mamade Issac always reached our place in the nick of time. We were informed of his arriving by the rattling sound of the last car from Grand-Baie to the vegetables market. The staggering cart was always behind the caravan because both the ox and the carter were old. As soon as the rattling sound of the cart were fainting the voice of the barber calling my father started echoing:

"*Chacha! Chacha!*"

    His calling was immediately accompanied by the barking of the blacksmith's dog opposite our house. That dog barked only at two persons. One was Mamade Issac himself and the other one was Soonooa, the obese of the locality. Once I heard my father joking and saying to Mamade Issac that the blacksmith's god might have been a near relative of the two in their previous lives.

    On that day, as always, my father's barber arrived at five in the morning with his small green coloured in valise and the bottle of hot water that even the customers of Ramduth coiffeur preferred to be shaved by Mamade. The children of all those houses, where the elders were the customers of Mamade Issac, were bound to have their hair cut by him. It was only in the evening that he came for the haircut. As requested by my father he returned for me on the same evening. He never reported to our houses for the haircut because the better accessible place for all was under the tamarind tree by our tabagie. All the children of the locality came to that very place to have their haircut. There was a specially mounted stone for that purpose on which I went to sit. He opened his green valise and took out the untidy apron like sheet and tied it around my neck. It was done to prevent us from getting pinched by the tiny pieces of the cut down hair lock going under the shirt.

I didn't like the way Mamade Issac sprinkled cold water on my head before starting his manoeuvre. His argument was that in order to give a proper cut the hair had to be wet. But there was one thing I liked with him and that was the way in which he would go on juggling the pair of scissors between his fingers throughout the haircut. And the thing I was much afraid of was his white razor with which he used to give a clean shave to the contours around the ears. He was never paid during the shaving of my father. Once every month I had to have my haircut and it was at that moment that his monthly account was settled and that monthly payment was of fifty cents. My elder friends had their coiffure done by Ramduth, the hairdresser. I also wanted to go to him but the cost at Ramduth's was almost the double. I wasn't at all satisfied by having my hair cut in Mamade Issac's "Pingo style". The elders were in a habit to laugh at us but to have our hairdresser changed was not an easy thing.

After the completion of Mamade's art on my head I went to my father. He opened the drawer and looked for a piece of 50 cents but when he couldn't find it he gave me instead two coins of twenty-five cents each. I took them to the barber, and as I was his last customer of the day he was packing up after cleaning his tools with the untidy apron. I handed him the two coins which he took to his pocket. While sliding them inside, one of the coins didn't reach his pocket. He was unaware of it. I wanted to tell him that one of his coins has fallen down but then remained quiet. In the morning I had been to the Chinese shop with my friends. Ismael and Hurrea had hunted a few centipedes from beneath stones and had them in a box of cigarettes. Madame Ah Moy used to buy those centipedes in order to use them to prepare her Chinese medicine. Her price for them would go from two to five cents each depending on the size. I was scared of those insects which brought 40 cents to my two friends on that day. They had then only 20 cents short for the tickets of the next day's matinee show. After having seen the huge poster of the Nadia and John Cavass starrer Hindi film, "*Flying Man*", I was as eager to go to the matinee show. With a very speedy heartbeat I watched Mamade Issac going away. On the soil beneath

Slices from a Life

the dried leaves of tamarind was still lying the coin. I stood there immobile watching the barber getting out of sight. I also had a glance in the direction of our tobacco shop. My father was busy chatting with Prasad Patya and Mahaveer Mahton, his two closest friends. I looked again at the coin. A thought came to me—'If I get it I'll be short of only five cents for the matinee show. And that five cents I can easily get either from my mother or my sister.' I bent down and with my two fingers picked up the twenty-five cents coin which I let it go straight in my trousers' pocket. Glimpses of tomorrow's film show started flickering in front of my eyes.

For most of my needs I happened to go first to my sister Tiffi. While going into the house I probed three or four times in my pocket and each time I was assured of having the ticket for "*Flying Man*" in my possession—with only five cents short. This question I could ponder upon even tomorrow morning because the show was to be in the afternoon but my eagerness after seeing the poster of the film rose to a crescendo. I decided first and foremost to go to my sister and be assured of getting the five cents I so badly needed. If in case I cannot get it from her I'll have to go to my mother in the morning and to cajole her. I went to Tiffi first. She was in the kitchen draining the rice. I said without any preface:

"You will have to give me five cents tomorrow."

Without taking away her eyes from the *degchi* she asked: "Why for?"

"All my friends are going to the cinema."

"Oh I see. . . but you need thirty cents for the ticket."

"I already have twenty-five cents with me. . ."

She looked at me. I fished out the coin from my pocket and showed to her. She asked me:

"Where did you get it from?"

"I found it on the road. . ."

"Tell me the truth. Where did you get this coin?"

I wasn't prepared for any such question from my sister. It was very difficult for me to maintain my lie in front of Tiffi. After putting aside the *degchi* she took hold of my hand holding the coin.

"Do tell me from where you got this twenty-five cents."

I remained silent and she repeated her question by scolding me. I told her the truth and bringing her voice to a lower tone she said:

"It wasn't expected of you. For this little piece of money Bhai Mamade Issac has to go to people at four in the morning even in the cold. You robbed him of a whole day's work."

"But *Didi* I didn't steal. . ."

"Stealing is still stealing; you have done the worse by taking possession of someone's labour. You have to return this to him. Bhai Mamade Issac is a very good man. You are not allowed to keep his hard-earned money."

The next morning when I was going to Mamade Issac I met him on the way. Giving him his money back I said:

"You had dropped it yesterday."

And before be could have said anything I ran back home. And it was only three weeks later that I got the opportunity of seeing the stunts of Nadia and John Cavass in the "*Flying Man*".

Encounter with the Wind

There used to be a world of difference between the temperaments of my mother and my father. My mother was too stingy with money and my father was a prodigal in squandering it away. My father lacked in self-confidence while my mother had it in plenty. My father was of hot temper and my mother the opposite of it. Despite his instant anger my father had hardly thrashed me and I can remember of only two instances when I was slapped by him. The first one was when on my way to our little tobacco shop with the plate of "*Nimkis*" (gâteaux pimentos) from our kitchen I dropped the plate. I was slapped by my father with the imprecation that it was a loss of two rupees because of my carelessness. The second instance was when I refused to wear the flabby trousers tailored by Adam, our village tailor. Coming to the number of times I was thrashed by my mother it becomes difficult to have them remembered because they were so many. The one reason of not remembering them was my mother's ways of having me cajoled two or three hours later after each thrashing. But still I remember of a few occurrences. The one being told here also shows my mother's willpower and self-confidence.

It was when I was eight or nine. The weather was very bad on that day and there were talks of the possibility of a cyclone among the village folks. On those days of school vacation I had the habit of running to the seaside with my friends. Sometimes we were for the whole day for which I was scolded and taken to task but it was all forgotten by me and the next day I again would join my friends for the swimming. On that day because of the bad weather my mother had warned me not to leave the house at all. A warning which I very easily forgot when I saw Jaddoo *Bhaiya's* oxcart proceeding to the Trou-aux-Biches area through the Kalimaye road. My two friends were already on the cart and it was indeed impossible for me to be left behind. I made a sudden swoop to the cart and holding the back part I jumped into it. The last three nights we had at our place the gathering of the women of our neighbourhood who helped my mother grinding '*Satwa*'—a mixture of maize, peas, pulse, lentils, rice, nuts and grams. Sitting around the *Jatta* they sang the *jantsar*, a special folksong for the purpose, till late in the night. Before going for fodder in the morning my mother kneaded the *Satwa* with milk and sugar. I had it in my both pockets wrapped in old newspaper. Throughout the journey I shared it with my friends.

We were in the midst of Fatima church and the Maheswurnath Temple where it started showering. The wind which had started much earlier was gradually becoming fierce. Jadoo *Bhaiya's* cart had to go to the plantation area so we three friends had to get down when the car turned to the right. We were almost to the sea and we completed our journey on foot in spite of the rain and the wind. We took off our clothes and leaving them under the coconut tree jumped into the sea. We were then carefree of the deteriorating weather. Someone going by the beach stopped and asked us not to swim bcause the waves were violent but we were not there to listen to anybody's advice. Gaffoor and Mohan were better swimmers than me and they were braver too. Forcing themselves against the roaring waves they had gone far enough from me. We were hardly in the water for an hour when Pitka, the watchman of Doctor Jhuboo who was the colleague of my father, saw us. After recognizing me he scolded me and ordered us to get out of water immediately:

"Do you want to die? All the boats of the fishermen are out of water and you are swimming in this bad weather! You all three get out of water immediately."

He ordered more loudly to Gaffoor and Mohan and we were all compelled to get out of water. Pitka didn't go to his bicycle which was leaning by a coconut tree until we didn't have our clothes on. He went his way only when we were on the way home. We were not at all in a hurry to reach home even in the rain and the increasing gusts. When I reached home my parents were already informed of our misdeed with much exaggeration—that if Pitka were not there to rescue us we would have been drowned. That was enough for my mother to grab me with one hand and slashing me with the other holding the rod. In a matter of moment I had all over my legs red marks, more painful after than at the time of the thrashing. That night I cried a lot – but not because of the physical pain. I cried for my mother. From the very approaching of the night the weather deteriorated to such an extent that what we started confrontating was a violent cyclone.

Our old house of wood and thatched roof started shaking like the trees outside. The termite-infested poles violently jerked by the wind were creaking. At each time my father expressed his anxiety and said that our house was going to be blown down. My mother with her self-confidence repeated telling us that it will not. With the advancing of the night the cyclone became more speedy and violent. Parts of the thatched roof of our house went on with the wind. All the three rooms were getting flooded by the leaking and splashing water. My little brother was though shrinked in my sister's lap. We were all scared. When the house began shaking more and more my mother said to my father:

"Take the children and go to Kadmi's house."

"And what about you?"

"I'll have to stay here."

My mother was confident that as long as she would be in the house it would not fall aground. Taking cover of my sisters, my father held me by my hand and my little brother in his lap got ready for shelter at Kadmi Phoophoo's house. Before leaving he once again said to my mum:

"It is not safe for you to stay alone here. The roof may come down any moment."

"As long as I'm here it will not come down."

The darkness was very dense outside. It was raining heavily. The speed of the gust was so terrible that going one step forward was difficult but we had to walk and reach our shelter before any tree or its branch falls on us. The thunder made us terror-stricken. Because of the lightning from time to time our way to Kadmi Phoophoo's house became slightly visible. The house stood on the other side of the road. It took us a long time enduring the dreary cyclone and reaching our refuge. The aloe fibre bag with which my father had covered my little brother was snatched away by powerful wind. We entered Phoophoo's house completely drenched. Being a new-built house there were other persons of the vicinity taking refuge there before us. Though it was a secured place I wasn't in a mood to feel myself secure, I was worried about my mum. The more violent became the cyclone the more perturbed I was. I started crying and calling my mother. I asked my father to go to our house and bring my mother along. I went on crying and imploring and at last my father went for her. Roopya *Didi*, our right side neighbour, was also there. She was praying and asking Hanumanji to have mercy on us and stop the cyclone. But the cyclone became excessively furious with the darkening night.

My father came back. My mother didn't want to leave the house still believing that no sooner than she leaves the house, it will collapse. I began crying again and wanted to go myself for my mother. I begged Phoophoo to come with me. Kadmi Phoophoo took hold of the cart lamp from the small wooden table and said to my dad:

"Let's go and see how she dares to stay there."

From time to time the wind became so strong. It seemed to us that even this new and strong house could not stand it. This made me more worry about my mother. I said to my sister:

"*Didi*, if our house comes down, my mother will die underneath."

If was after a long half an hour Phoophoo and my father came back with my mother between them. I ran to her and she took me in her embrace. Kadmi Phoophoo then told us that they hardly walked a few steps from our house when its roof came down. The light of the hurricane in Phoophoo's hand was dead. I was still in the embrace of my mother when the thought came to me – 'Was it really the self-confidence of my mother that stopped the house from coming down until she was in or does it really happen that as long as a member of the house stays in, it can resist the cyclone?'

Slices from a Life

Berries Sweet and Sour

The Maheshwurnath Temple's atrium in those days was without fencing and had a wide expanse. It had on one side the mango orchard and on the other a wide plain. Along the plain there used to be a widely spread banyan tree with very dense network of hanging roots. Behind the huge banyan tree was the ruin of an old sugarcane mill. It was the time when the very popular film *"Tarzan"* was running at Anand, the village cinema hall. Along with my friends I had seen Johnny Weissmuller in the role of Tarzan. My friends and I tried to imitate him by swinging from one hanging root of the banyan to another and thus by going through three to four roots we jumped either on the ground or went straight on the top of the grey stones of the ruin. The most agile of all of us were Ravin and Gaffoor. The speed with which they used to swing from one hanging root to the other and the height they reached to before catching the next root were never surpassed by any one of us. This was not accepted by Mahen who was the lousiest of all who always pretended to be the real Tarzan amongst us. He was the most canny and always mischievous. It was he who once went to the cane field and told Parsad that his house was burgled. Parsad reached his house running and panting to know that he was made a fool by Mahen. Very often Mahen would play such ugly game which, to all of us, was great fun.

There was a berry tree in the ruin behind the dense surrounding of the banyan. There were several berry trees around the Shivala but the one in the ruin bore the sweetest and the plumpest berries in the locality. During the fruit season all the children remained clung to that very tree and coped with each other to reach for the plumpest berries. Gaffoor and Ravin were capable of going up to the top to get possession of the choicest. Mahen wasn't pleased at all and

Slices from a Life

it was much of a regret to me that I couldn't make it to reach the top of the tree. Another reason for my frustration was because of the temptation provoked by Gaffoor and Ravin. They would take out selected berries out of their pockets during our swinging on the hanging roots of the banyan or while we happened to play football made of tattered garments. With mischief in both their eyes and smiles they would make great show of their selected ones before eating them. Mahen and I were hardly in agreement, we would fight with each other on banal issues. It was one of the rare occasions when I agreed to sit with him and find out ways and means to solve the problem concerning the monopoly of the two experts on the best berries. We went away from our friends and sat under a tree in the mango orchard and started thinking of an easy device in order to have our shares of the chosen berries.

The fruit had just started ripening. We knew that the berries would be in maturity and fully juicy in a matter of days and all the children would pounce on the tree. Mahen came with an idea to have some of the strong boys in our side so that with some scuffling we could have our exclusive right on the berry tree. I didn't like the idea. After brooding over the matter for long enough I said to Mahen:

"We must think of a way to keep others away from the tree."

It made Mahen rebound and he immediately said,

"I got it."

"Do tell me how!"

"You said of keeping them away from the tree?"

"Yes. But how can we do it?"

"Ok, you be quiet and let me do the rest. As from tomorrow nobody will approach the tree."

I couldn't believe him so easily because I knew of his verbosity and yet on that day I stayed with him till late. By five in the afternoon when all the children getting enough of the day started going back home I remained with Mahen. His house was at a stone's throw. He was the son of the Shivala's priest. I went with him up to his house. Mahen's father happened to be my Guru because of my having the sacred thread ritual by him. I was scared to be in front of him so I stayed behind the mango tree. The reason of my being nonplussed was because of the so-talked-about enchanting practices of his. People used to come to him from far away places for magic cure. Mahen went inside the house and some ten minutes later came back to me with something wrapped in an old newspaper. When I asked him what it was, he just said:

"Follow me."

We went straight to the ruin. The afternoon was running away with great speed in order to make room for the night. Duskiness was spreading. We reached the tree of sweetest berries of the area. Mahen unwrapped the content in his hand. He took out four pieces of camphor and put them by the roots of the tree. He lighted them and picking up pinches of vermilion from the still half folded newspaper; he marked the trunk of the tree on several places with the vermilion powder. I tried to understand the performance taking place which I really understood when on the next day Mahen addressed all the boys gathered under the Banyan in the following words:

"The berry tree amidst the ruin is occupied by a shrew. Yesterday at dusk in the form of a woman she tried to strangle me."

And then pointing at me he continued:

"The shrew released my neck when she saw him."

The children looked at me. According to what has been decided between Mahen and me I had to add my yes to his yes. I did it. The eyes of all our friends were reflecting a sudden fear. Mahen went on with his story.

"The shrew after lighting camphor near the tree said that she will suck the blood of whoever will try to approach the tree."

Gaffoor was the only one to remain unconvinced by the story but when he went to the berry tree and saw for himself the stain of camphor and marks of *sindoor* on the tree he started advising everyone not to go near the tree. He reminded the children of Ramdeva's misfortune how he was caught by a shrew and became mad for ever. Our stratagem was a success.

In a few days the berries started getting ripening in plenty. Mahen and I went to the tree in hiding and rejoiced ourselves of the selected berries for many days. Our friends were scared even to look in the direction of the tree. Whenever someone happened to share a few berries with his friend, he was asked of the tree from which the fruit came before being accepted. Our tactics went on successfully the next year also but the moment Ravin along with two other friends detected upon us and caught both of us on the tree savouring the forbidden berries it was the end of our exclusivity and as before the sweet berries were turned into sour ones.

Amongst the Don Juans

Being cheated or fooled by friends is like being disgraced. But there are moments that, when nonplussed or brought into the ridicule by friends, provide a feeling of intimacy. They give a sort of pleasure rather than pain. I have on many occasions come accros both emotional experiences. Sometimes I have been deeply hurt by the ruggedness of some of my friends and often shared with them their enjoyment. I was of a very frail body and perhaps the most stupid of them that was the reason of my being ridiculed by them so often. When it comes to the teasing of girls I used to keep myself at arm's length, because of my timid nature. In spite of it complaints of teasing girls never ceased reaching my place. And it was all the time done on purpose by my friends. Those experts in teasing girls of the locality were Premwa, Bidyanan and Mohanwa. They teased the girls and I was scolded at home. I was, on a few occasions, thrashed for it. My sister who was aware of my friends' behaviour said to me:

"You are made to be accountable for their deeds because of your silliness."

My mother in a very different tone would say, as for example:

"Mohan also is of your age but how is it that nobody points any accusing finger at him?"

Once the story had a twist of its own. No complaint reached my parents but when I reached home it was to face shame and bewilderment at the same time. It was the day of Mahashivratri. The Maheshwarnath Temple's atrium was crowded with devotees from several villages and towns. It was a time when loudspeaker was just introduced in village celebrations. Though the fast sound coming from the loudspeaker was unbearable to the ears my friends and I were very close to it, listening the *bhajan*. It was Mohan who, pointing at a slim girl with very long hair, said to me by bringing his mouth very close to my ear:

"That girl has her eyes glued on you and you pretend to be unaware. Go closer to her you stupid, and try to smile at least."

Prem and Bidya joined him to prompt me. Encouraged by them I went closer to the girl with the long hair and started roaming around with a difficult smile. She was with her parents, and looked like someone from town in her beautiful white garb. At the time when I happened to be at a distance from her, my three friends started inciting me and I after mustering courage again and went on keeping closeness with my borrowed smile. It had no effect on her. After the *puja* when she along with her parents left the temple's courtyard for the busstand the four of us went behind them. In those days the terminus was at Neuvieme Mille, after leaving our house. Suddenly I was stunned by what happened. I saw the girl with the long hair and her parents entering our courtyard. I got a chilling premonition of something unpleasant. My three friends with their silent steps went their way. I couldn't understand what was happening. But then I came to know it when still with fearing steps I entered our house through the back door. I was told by my sister that the girl was the daughter of a cousin of mine from Port Louis. It was the first time that I saw them. Asked by my mother I went to the other room to meet and greet them. The girl with the long hair who was supposed to be my niece looked at me with a side-glance and smiled mischievously. Nevertheless it was a relief for me of not being reported and also a pledge not to tease girls anymore or at least to know about the girl first before approaching her.

The second event concerning this going to and fro around girls has another crisp denouement. In other words it is another sharp example of my dullness. We had no bicycle at our place when I was in my early teens. It was the irony of fate because prior to my birth the house had the first car in the locality. I was very fond of riding bicycle and had to borrow it from friends. In the afternoon, boys, back from the sugarcane fields, were in the habit of having as footwear wooden sandals known as *kharpa* and Himalayan snow cream in their faces to go out roaming. Prem was supposed to be the most elegant among my friends with his vaselined head. He had a new Raleigh cycle which no one was allowed to touch. That afternoon I also had a cycle in my possession.

I am not so sure, it might have belonged either to Dayanand or Dadibal, my two other friends. Invited by Premwa I went with him for a ride to the other side of our village. His cycle was equipped with both a bell and a horn. He was wearing a black sunglass, of course not to have him protected from the sun. At that period there used to be public taps throughout the road always surrounded by girls and women with their buckets and pails. At every fountain-gathering Premwa, in order to attract the attention of the girls, hooted the cycle horn and rang the bell, simultaneously.

The sunshine had already started losing brightness when we entered a narrow lane at the Cinéma Cassé. Prem's cycle was more speedy and he himself was more at ease with it owing to which I was left behind from time to time. We reached a tap where some four or five girls were gathered for water. Premwa started hooting and ringing; then began whistling and winked one of his eyes at the girls. The local cinema was showing "*Panna*", a film by Jairal and Geeta Nizami at that time. When Prem reached near the girls he said to one of them:

"Hello my *Panna*! My darling!"

We rode to a certain distance from the public tap and then made a U turn. Then suddenly Prem stopped and came down of his Raleigh. He took my cycle and gave his new one to me. He also gave me his dark sunglass which I immediately took to my eyes. While returning when we arrived near the tap we saw some people standing by. We were both stopped by them. A girl among them pointed at me and said:

"It is he who called me darling and '*Panna*'".

In the meantime Prem managed to go far enough from the angry crowd. What could have been my state? You can just imagine it if you have ever been of that age of nine. It is said that foolish sometimes have luck. At that very moment the eldest of the girls came forward and before the angry people would have started taking me to task she shouted:

"It was the other one who teased us."

Slices from a Life

Monday Was Not a Holiday

It was my fourth year in the primary school. All the attractions and attachment I had for the school have started fading in these three and a half years. The nearly a mile distance to Maheshwurnath Aided School which in the beginning we used to complete in merriment seemed longer with time. Even the school yard has lost its fervour and the joy of a certain freedom we used to have in the earlier days of standards one to three has vanished. Mr. Bissessur, our teacher of Std IV, was a slim man and was as serious as severe. His shining rattan rod was most of the time in his hand than on the upper part of the blackboard. He was never in the least worried about the spoiling of the rod. On every third or fourth day he happened to have a new "*rotin bazar*". He was in the habit of saying that he had to let the rods get spoiled so often in order to spare the children from getting spoiled.

It was because of the seriousness of our teacher and his "*timimi*", the rattan stick, that the eagerness we had to reach school in the three earlier years had disappeared. We had to look for excuses not to go to school. The usual pretexts of headache and stomach pain were no more accepted by our parents. My mother wouldn't like me to look for any excuse to abstain from school. She said:

"You lose seven days of study by abstaining a single day."

A quite number of pupils in our class were disheartened because of the atmosphere in the classroom. Many of us were more scared of Mr Bissessur's wrath than his rod. We were three boys from the extreme north of the village sharing the same class and the fear. My two friends were much more scared than me amongst whom Taleb was a dead hand in providing pretexts. His parents were easily convinced of his headaches and other pains. He very easily did succeed in keeping himself away from school twice or thrice per week. Whenever I borrowed excuses from him they went in vain. One afternoon looking for an excuse for the next day, I showed to my mother the blue scars on my palm left by the slashing of the "*rotin bazar*" to which she said:

"These are inflictions to make children more attentive."

I wanted to go to the seaside with Taleb the next day but the excuse wasn't cashed by my mother. Taleb always tempted me with his sea-side adventures, his fishing, swimming and running after crabs. I could do nothing than wishing to have been born in his house where excuses were so easily believed. The walking distance from my house to the school was of half an hour owing to which we were not able to reach the school when it rained heavily. Every time when we did not want to go to the school we wished that it rains cats and dogs. It was Taleb himself who had taught us some tactics. One of them was to sing a few lines of "*harparowri*", a folksong to implore the rain god Indra which we have learnt from the old women of the locality. But the rain god paid no heed to our imploration. We had to opt for another mode. We sat on the ground and one of us would draw a circle on the dusty soil; then in unison we would say "*Jam ke baras pani jam ke baras*"—O rain, fall! Fall in torrents and non-stop. One of us would bring a pebble and after splitting around it put it in the circle. But even this fantastic trick never brought any rain for us.

But that specific day of the event that followed was a day after a torrential rain. Unfortunately, the raining day was not of any advantage to us who were so yearning for a heavy rain. It was so because the raining day was a Sunday. In those days there was a ditch in the back of our thatched roof house which remained overflowed with rain water even after three or four days. I had only two suits combined of trousers and shirts being both my home dress and school's. When one was being worn by me the other one was washed and made ready to replace. I did come to notice that the one I wore on Friday was just washed and streched on a rope to get dry. Going to school on Mondays was usually a very hard nut to crack to me. Having seen one of my suits still soacked on the rope, an idea to stay at home clicked my mind. I was made to get ready for school, only after my mother's return with the first trip of fodder for our two cows. In between the two suits I had to stay indoors in a ragged piece of cloth. After handing me my second suit and ordering me to get ready for school immediately she went to complete some of her everyday commitments before going to the second fodder trip. I put on the clothes and came out. Avoiding being spotted by my mother and sister I went straight to the ditch full of the rain water. With a gesture as though I had slipped I let myself fall in the ditch and started screaming. My sister followed by my mother came to me and it was my sister who holding my hand pulled me out. My clothes were completely drenched with muddy water.

My mother very often perceived the reality in a flash. She told my sister that the act was done deliberately by me in order to abstain from school. Another reason of her guessing the truth was because of my own fault. Last night when my father was telling me the story of "*Belwanti Rani*", the enchanted fairy queen, my mother asked him more than once to postpone the story for next night and to let me go to bed so that I can get up early in the morning for school. I wanted my father to continue the story and insisted on not going to school next day. My mother took my hand from my sister's hold and scolded me:

"I'm going to see how you do not go to school."

There was still half-hour time to leave for school. My mother stood by me and compelled me to get myself rid of the clothes full of mud. She gave me an "*orhni*" of my sister to cover myself and in the meantime took out my wet clothes from the rope. She went to the kitchen and holding the clothes over the flames of the oven heated then until they were half dried. I had to wear them and unwillingly I did proceed to school. That night my mother made a mixture of hot milk, saffron and "*citronella*" and gave me to drink. It was to keep me safe from catching pneumonia because of the wet clothes I had on me for almost half the day at school.

The Fast U-turn

My father addressed him as Lamka Deoduth because he was tall and slim but I had to call him uncle. He was from Fond du Sac and used to come to our village with a big bundle of clothes to sell around to the villagers. Being our relative most of the time he left his bundle in our custody. He was a happy-go-lucky person whom the village children were very fond of. He would talk for long moments with my friends and me. Sometimes in his good mood he would tell us stories of gallant heroes and their bravery and he would also teach us religious and patriotic songs. On other occasions he made us laugh by telling us of hilarious events. He was very good at versification and was a very good friend of Karim Mamoo because they had a common habit. Once when near the Kalimaye Karim Mamoo asked him why the children of the locality were so fond of him, he said in his usual rhyming—

"*Baché howé man ké saché, panhchanté hein admi aché.*— The children are pure of heart and they easily recognise a good man."

One day he came to us with a basket full of bananas. I was sitting on the large rock under the mango tree in front of our house. He came to me and said:

"*Aré beté kahé baithé akélé. Awo khalo kelé ban jawo merré chélé.*—Why are you sitting alone? Join me and let us finish with these bananas."

Deoduth *Chacha* always had rhymes on his lips which we enjoyed very much and up to such an extent that one of us, Gowtam, started imitating him. One midday, when in the blazing sun he put his bundle on his head to start his work my father said:

"*Eissan gham mé kam?*—Working in this blazing sun?"

To which he gave the instant reply:

"*Kam hi mé howe Ram, chaon howé ya gham.*—In work itself God is found—be it shade or the sun."

There were so many rhyming sentences which my friends and I went on repeating but there remains one instance which

Slices from a Life

I cannot forget. Both the instance and the two rhyming sentences were uttered by Deoduth *Chacha*.

It started one afternoon from the Hindi School at Neuvième Mille. Deoduth *Chacha* took hold of us and made us accompany him to the *Baithka* where some two hundred persons had already assembled. The workers' leader they were all waiting for turned up after a long hour. He delivered a long speech in Bhojpuri and reminded everybody that the peaceful protest against alcohol which had already started was going to have its most meaningful stage. And thus it was fixed for Saturday, that was three days after. He also told his silent listeners that on the occasion a procession would start at 7 sharp in the morning from Cottage. Passing through several villages it would reach Triolet by 9 o'clock. People would join the procession from every village and the time it reaches Terre Rouge, the rendezvous for the peaceful demonstration, the number should reach to ten thousand. Other processions would also be coming from other parts.

"We have to show and convince the government that the effect of alcohol in the society is becoming more and more serious. The workers are spending the lion's share of their income on drinking and leaving their family in dire straits."

The whole crowd was very much influenced by the oration and clamoured:

"*Mazdoor Zindabad! Sharab Murdabad!*
Long live the workers! Death to alcohol!"

Villagers of Triolet, particularly those of our areas, started preparing placards with anti-alcohol slogans for the coming demonstration. Every bit of work was being supervised by Deoduth *Chacha*. My friends and I started giving a helping hand. We were told that the involvement of the youths and the children would prove to the authority that prohibition had become a must. I was given the charge of writing a placard in Hindi which read—"Man drinks the alcohol and the alcohol drinks the man". Several placards with different readings were ready overnight. When my father caught me scribbling he warned me:

"It's alright you can help your *Chacha* but mind you! You will not form part of the procession."

I said nothing. My friends and I had decided that none of us would let his parents know of our active participation. In the afternoon after relating to us some stories of bravery

Slices from a Life

Deoduth *Chacha* said:

"Children have to be courageous and fearless. He who will be afraid will reach nowhere—*Himmat karo kismat banao, Darogé to rowogé*...Have courage and be successful, get afraid and remain crying."

On the day of the peaceful demonstration we avoided the sight of our parents and went at a distance from our houses prior to the arrival of the procession. We waited for the caravan started from Cottage to come. After a long period of waiting we saw the procession coming afar. When it approached we heard the song and the slogans of the marchers who were repeating after Deoduth *Chacha's* clamour:

"*Sharab hé kharab*!
Alcohol is detrimental!
Nashakhodi band ho!
We want prohibition!"

The marchers were being led by *Chacha* who asked us to join them. One after another we entered the rows and joined the chorus:

"Long live the workers! Down with alcohol. People were joining us from every nook and corner. I was very close to Deoduth *Chacha* and was walking in accordance with his steps. It was decided amongst us that we cannot go up to Terre Rouge but at least we will accompany the procession up to Solitude. After completing a three-mile march we were to arrive near the Bassin Mervin of Solitude when suddenly the caravan came to a halt. Deoduth *Chacha* turned to the marchers and brandishing his fist said:

"*Rookogé to jhookogé, jhookogé to katogé aur marogé*. March on! We have already completed two thirds of our journey."

He was still addressing the marchers and boosting their morale when someone coming from the direction of the reservoir shouted:

"Stop! The police is barricading."

We all looked to the direction showed by the intruder and saw several policemen with batons and guns coming in our direction. The crowd was still on move when suddenly the unexpected occurred. The procession was brought to a halt.

Deoduth *Chacha* was moving away. Detaching himself

from the crowd he said,

"*Ab toom log jawo maré Deoduth jayé gharé* (—Now you all go to hell, I'm going back home)."

In the late afternoon we came to know that at Solitude no police interception took place but at the railway station of Terre Rouge the demonstrators were surrounded by police with batons and tear gas. There were also firing and many people were either wounded or taken prisoner. Deoduth *Chacha* who made the fast U-turn didn't turn up for weeks. And for weeks I suffered the pang of guilt for being a deserter, though unwillingly.

In the Midst of Poets and Politicians

Sitting on the same podium along with politicians has always been some sort of an allergy to me of which I cannot blame myself. It's a natural ailment one cannot be accountable for. One may be allergic even of beautiful carpets or flowers and perfumes. Despite your knowledge of the fact that certain flowers are bound to give us bronchial and other problems, we are deliberately or undeliberately around them. In spite of the awareness that sharing a cultural or literary platform with politicians has always been painful to me, it hasn't been always easy to avoid the persisting requests of the organisers. I have known very less such compromises and one among them happened to be a function at the Town Hall of Curepipe which I am going to relate here. My memory being not so clear about the exact date of the event, it may be in the month of December around 1980.

The members of Hindi Lekhak Sangh and Hindi Chatra Sangh came to invite me to a recital of poems by Mauritian poets. As usual, I kept insisting that I cannot afford to be on the same podium with politicians but the obstinacy of the organisers happened to strike a more stubborn posture. I accepted the invitation on the condition that I'll speak a few words but will not read any poem of mine. I did accept the request because of the good initiative of the organisers who took Hindi poetry from the villages to the town hall.

It was indeed a well organised function. When I reached there, the place was houseful. People in eagerness were waiting for the arrival of the Prime Minister, the Minister of Education and others. My friend Pandit Dharamveer Ghura was one of the organisers. I was talking to some friends around when, with two other members of the organising committee, Pandit Ghura came to me. After taking me a few steps away from my friends, he said to me very pleadingly:

"We request you please at least today do not speak against

the politicians".

Seeing his facial expression and the way he implored, I was bound to smile, I said smilingly:

"Don't worry. I'll not be an obstacle to your coming promotion."

The political personalities started coming one after another and were taken with due respect on the stage. The Prime Minister, Sir Seewoosagur Ramgoolam, was the last person to arrive and yet he was five minutes earlier of the scheduled time. As usual, he didn't go straight to the stage; instead in his way, he went on talking with all those persons known and unknown. He reached the podium in time. I was given a seat beside him. While the secretary was briefing the Prime Minister about the programme, I cast a glance at those sitting down the stage in front of us and then looked at the eminent ones on the stage. Out of the ten, seven were politicians. The ten poets participating in the recital were sitting down on their chairs and were looking happy enough to occupy the first row.

The person conducting the programme informed us that there will be only four brief speeches and after that the recital of poems will take place. Some twenty minutes went on garlanding the politicians. On my arrival, I had tried to convince the organisers to have only one speech by the Prime Minister and then go straight for the recital but then I learned that pleasing the Minister of Education and two other ministers was the leitmotif of the whole show. I was given the floor to start the speech part of the programme. The poets sitting in front of us, instead of sharing the stage, were giving me a sort of uneasiness. I wanted to start my speech by disapproving the policy but I was reminded of the promise I made to my friends not to provoke the wrath of the politicians. So I couldn't let things go against the organisers. Pandit Ghura was sitting in the front row among the poets and seemed to be silently warning me of any slip of tongue.

I found myself in a vortex of circumstances. I was thinking of ways and means to speak out of the thing that was not pleasing me at all. I started my formal speech with dilemma inside my mind—to say it or not. I knew that saying it would not go in favour of the organisers, but not saying was letting the poets insulted and that was suffocation to me. It was a recital of poems but the poets were not given their deserving place on the podium. They were supposed to come on stage one by one after hearing their names, read their poems respectively, and go back.

I neither wanted to embarrass my friends of the organising side, nor let my friends of the literary world humiliated in that way. After a brief speech of quarter an hour on literacy trend, I had a pause and looked at the audience in front of me and then the two directions of stage. Those of the audience who were expecting, as usual, something explosive from me were looking disappointed. But they knew that the speech was not yet over. I cast a second glance at them and as though addressing to the Prime Minister, I said very calmly:

"I regret only one thing in this function. The politicians have been given the seats of the poets and the poets are sitting in the places of the politicians."

There were clappings and no clapping. Returning to my seat, I saw the Prime Minister talking in the ear of the Minister of Education. The next moment, the Minister of Education whispered something in the ears of the organiser and, in matters of moment, some ten chairs were arranged on the stage. This time, the Secretary spoke very briefly:

"Now, I have the honour to ask the Minister of Education to say a few words."

The Minister of Education went to the mike and addressing the poets said:

"I request all the poets who are down the stage to please come on the stage. You take your seats first and after that, I'll be speaking a few words."

All the poets responded to the invitation of the Minister and came on the stage. After the speech of the Prime Minister, the poets recited their poems. At the end, everybody gathered for tea during which most of the audience talked about what took place. Some of them looked at me as though I was a victor, others seemed to disapprove my mischief. And I heard one of them saying:

"Abhimanyu wasn't happy because he didn't get a garland."

Slices from a Life

My Addiction for Comics

It was during 1950 and 51. Though being a slow coach in my class I was able to pass the Std. VI exams, (of course with very narrow margin) and got my admission to the Neo College in Port Louis. The college had just moved from Conti Street to a multistoreyed building in La rue Madame. It was a college mostly frequented by students from the north parts of the island. I had to leave my village on Mondays and after a stay of four nights at my sister's house in the Maupin Street, I used to come back to my village home for the weekends. Most of the students travelled by train but because of no railway facility from Triolet to Port Louis, I had to make it by bus along with my friend Jawahurlal. My friend also had to stay at his cousin's, situated in the premises of the Government House, for his schooling. The bus fare for school children was twenty cents for one way trip and yet our parents were not in a position to pay for our everyday tickets.

Staying away from bosom friends for four to five days per week was indeed painful but then it did not take much time for the two of us and our classmates to become intimate. In order to reach my sister's house from the college I had to take the Orleans Street and either from La rue Dechartre or Condé to cross the Moka Street. Amongst my new friends at the college who had to do the same course to reach their houses were Heeralall Bhugaloo, Michel Dedans, Amadis Jhuboolal Hosseny and others. We preferred going through the canal and under the bridge instead of going by road. Michel Dedans and Amadis were supposed to be living in the vicinity of Condé Street and Heeralal Bhugaloo, in La rue d'Entrecasteaux. The canal coming from the east of the Madame Street and passing in front of our college to cross the Moka Street was always full of water. The newcomer chock-stick 'sorbet' had already become a craze among the students. After our treat with the sorbet we used to retain the flat stick and write our names on it respectively. On our way back home all of us were ready for the regatta and would slowly drop our stick boats on the water stream and follow the race. We were from five to seven to compete with. And each of us was a winner in turns.

A few of us were also in the habit of mutually exchanging comics. Despite my daily saving of the five cents as the limited sum of my 'tiffin', I was capable of buying only one comics magazine per month. My friends showed certain hesitation in lending me their new acquired one because with only two or three issues in my collection I was not able to cope with them in the mutual exchange. The first comics I bought with my pocket money was "*The Phanthom*" costing forty cents. The first book that it brought me in exchange from one of my friend was '*Bibi Fricotin*'. Lured by this revelling reading I yearned to have in my possession as many comics and books of stories told in pictures. At noon when everybody was having the treat of his tiffin, I kept my daily five cents in pocket to buy those reading and entertaining stuffs yet could not cope with my friends. But then, as said that every cloud has a silver lining, came the days when I started having some money of my own.

With time, life in town had started becoming interesting enough, still I waited for Fridays with great eagerness. My sister was a very good cook but she had not got the dexterity of my mother's cuisine. My eagerness had other reasons too. In those days very few students from villages joined colleges in the towns and villages didn't have colleges at all. Hardly four or five students travelled with me from Triolet. Even the rich people were not interested in sending their children for secondary education. The other reason of my eagerness to return home was because of those four-five families where I was so badly needed. They were families of those in the Royal Pioneer Corps serving for the British cause in Egypt. The women of these far away soldiers used to come at my place in weekends to have their letters written. Besides writing letters on their behalf to their husbands I had also to read for them their received ones which were most of the time in Bhojpuri and Creole written in Roman script.

The most regular amongst these few women were Bibi Rabia, the wife of Moostoof Bhai, Ramdeo's wife Dulareea and the mother of Koodoos. They were also the most kind. The others also did give me a few cents for service rendered, on the "Fête Caba's" days but the three mentioned above were more generous by giving me up to one rupee. At the end of every month the families of the soldiers serving abroad were given a pension by the Government which was known as "Fête Caba". They had to collect it from Port Louis office and for that special day the car of my friend Hossen Edun's father Bhai Hamja was ever booked in advance. Triolet had hardly four or five cars at that time. The allowance day was indeed a glamorous day for which I had the same impatience as that of those entitled for it. My share was an overall of three to four rupees per month. What a big sum for me to spend over my so cherished comics magazines! I bought them from Librairie Sénèque in Sir William Newton Street. The beautiful cashier of the library was all the time very conscious of not letting her with white coloured hand to get touched by those of the payers.

In the vicinity of Neo College there were a few loitering youngsters who always tried to cow down the students coming from villagers. Once when I was coming straight from Triolet three of them stopped me and taking possession of my bag took away all my books and magazines, not sparing me of the few cents I had with me. This was not the first incident. My other friends were already their victims. The students from villages who were in upper classes decided to put an end to the dirty game. The two gangs confronted and the village students were successful in compelling the loiterers to show their clean pair of heels. After that no such incident ever took place but our principal Mr D. Nepal restricted the circulation of comics among the students. Despite the ban we continued with it in hiding. When I reached the form two my parents were once again put to dire straits as a result of which I had to stop myself from going to college. Even in that tight situation my mother tried all her level best to make me continue with my education but my decision was to face the scarcity. I had no alternative than to join my labourer friends in the sugarcane fields. It was from that moment that my addiction for comics was put to a stop. And my love for Hindi books started.

Memento of Unemployed Days

The present has to get rid of the past in order to survive and for the sake of future the present has to die. In those days I was bound to think that way. I had completed my sixteen. Difficult days have raised to such a crescendo of helplessness that my mother, who was fighting tooth and nail to have my education continue, has to give up. Her earnest desire to make of me a someone with white-collar job has vanished and her dream dashed to pieces. The forest and the reserved land around for fodder having been converted into plantation tending the cows had become as though fighting a crusade. Over all this we had our debt and dire straits at its worst. My father, because of his illness, was bed-ridden.

My nights went away thinking about how I could be helpful in the livelihood of the six members in our house. My abandoned sister with her child has come to make our burden heavier. Because of my sleepless nights I was a late riser and my mother, seeing me on the bed after sunrise, would shout forth in anger:

"You the laziest of all! Will you go on sleeping the whole day? For how long I'll have to struggle for someone of your age?"

She started mentioning the names of those of my age living around and went on saying:

"They are younger than you. They are earning. How could I afford to let you live the life of a prince doing nothing?"

I had become used to it. Her prompt anger was as flashy as the thunder. Her bitterness was very superficial and yet I was both put to shame and pained by the everyday scolding. It was for more than six months that I had to swallow those reprimands along with the thin meals of everyday. Even in the evenings before the dinner I was served with the same

Slices from a Life

appetizer. On one or two occasions I had to leave my food and go away but then I had to blame myself for the prevailing situation. I came to the conclusion that my mother had all the right to behave that way. For how long she could have let me sit at home doing nothing when the cow and the goats in our stable were themselves underfed. My mother could not have done otherwise than shower all her anger on me.

I have started feeding up with that present of mine. I had no future in its existence but it was also difficult for me to kill that present. I had to go on chewing it like an already chewed gum. My education had come to a stop because of lack of means. The work which I had started in the sugar estate despite my frail body had to be given up because of the harshness of the estate owner on whom I had to throw my bill hook. Several of my friends were happy-go-lucky boys. I wanted to dress and behave like them.

On that particular afternoon after asking for something to eat for more than once I had to press my stomach with Sharat Chandra's "*Chareetraheen*" which I was reading. But when unable to appease the hunger I started reading the novel again, but could not find the refuse I was so wanting. In my concentration to seek that refuse I was not aware of my sister coming and leaving the *thali* of rice by me. I don't know I might have seen her and yet in my anger had deliberately ignored the plate of food.

Later on, when my mother saw the food untouched and myself plunged in reading shouted at me:

"It is *dal* and fried *brede mourome.* What more do you want me to provide?"

Mother's remark didn't have any pain-giving intention and yet for reasons unknown to myself a few drops came out of my eyes and were blotted by the open page of the novel in my hand.

My mother was still repeating her reproach from the other room:

"With no work at this age; all the time sitting and reading: . . . As though you have to become Balmiki. . ."

Tears were on the verge to come out of my eyes but I suppressed them; but not for long. Drops dripped down again on the pages and I closed the book to have them preserved.

Weeks back the book was returned to the oriental shelves of the Mauritius Institute Library from where it was loaned;

but it was impossible to return those drops to its place from where they dropped down.

Several years after that painful event I went into the Mauritius Institute Library. It was by mere chance that while looking for a Hindi book among the limited number of Hindi books of the library that I came across the novel with drops of my tears on its pages. I took the book which was unread for a long time in my hands and started turning the pages as though I was looking for something hidden among them. And suddenly those two pages were so near to my eyes on which were treasured those drops, memento of my unemployed days. The idea of taking away the book from there came to me but then rejected for I realized that the souvenir was in the proper place.

I did shed those tears on my corpse by killing my present to be able to possess that future which is today my present and which is to be my past tomorrow—but for ever my present.

Winning the Race and Losing Face

It's the time when some people talked of the last race of the year as "Lé Coursé Malbar". And for that purpose special holiday was allotted to the workers of the sugar industry and the labourers and other workers were in a sort compelled to rush for it. Despite the terrible plight they had to face in the streets of Port-Louis and at the Champ-de-Mars these village folks make it a must to attend the races. They came in buses, trains and even by oxcarts, packed to capacity with their whole family. For this rare joy of their life they had to undergo routine humiliation which used to be more painful than that of the oppression during the working time in the sugarcane fields.

The traffic in those days was so irregular on the main road of Triolet that a car or a bus was seen at intervals of almost half an hour. Oxcarts were then to be seen more than those vehicles. Almost for the whole day the still road was used as playground by the children of the locality. They felt at ease to play either Football or "*Kabaddi*" in the mid of the road. We cleared the road only when the sound of a far coming car came to our ears or when one of our friends would raise his voice to warn us of any approaching vehicle. The event that follows took place when the movements of Pandit Beessoondoyal and Pandit Ramnarain were on their culminating points. One was struggling for the revival of culture and language and the other for the right of workers and social justice.

In spite of the constant instructions and warnings by the two leaders of Jan Sangh and Majdoor Sangh the workers of the sugar estate made it a must to rush for the so-called "Lé Course Malbar". They very easily forgot the humiliation of the year before and joined the caravan. The Jan Andolan and the Majdoor Andolan both had a great influence on the people of my village and yet many and even a few fervent ones reached the Champ-de-Mars as early as possible. In order to prevent these village folks from going to that disgracing fair and to spare their children and women from being disgraced a vegetables seller by the name of Motee, and widely known as "Garrison", took the challenge.

Many people, as excuse, would say that they went to that race because of their children; so what Motee did was to create an attraction for the children. On the very day of the "Dernier Les Courses", he organized running competition for children which became popular overnight.

Runners were selected in three different categories. Everyone had to enter the group according to one's age. The parents would line themselves on both sides of the road to watch their children's performance. The group I had to join was that of the under-fifteen. In the first two years I came as fourth and third and was satisfied of my little progress. For the third place I was given the prize of one rupee by the organizer. On both occasions I had as rivals Jawahur and Dayananad. Both of them were very fast runners. Jawahur was the faster and he was given the nickname of "Toofan Mail": those were the days of films by Nadia and Jon Cavas.

For the third competition Jawahur moved to the superior group and that gave me more confidence to overtake Dayanand who was faster than me in the group. The formalities of the competition always started as from eleven in the morning to be completed by quarter to two in order to enable the runners to stand by for the first race due to start at two in the afternoon and end at five. All the prizes of the first two categories were of seven rupees each and for the remaining firsts it was five rupees for each winner. I was confident of winning the second prize of my category if not the first one. But I was badly interested for the first prize of five rupees because the key-winding tank I had seen at Michel's shop had a tag of five rupees on it.

The preparations had started at eleven sharp and by twelve I already had my number which I went to show my sister and promised her to come first. We were in all eight groups of runners. The distance of the first three groups was the same — that is of six hundred metres. I belonged to the four hundred metres groups. The departure line was as always vis-à-vis Garrison's house. My group had to go up to

Kalimaye near the Public Fountain and make a U-turn while those of the first team had to go up to "La Boutique Paul" and back. My number was five and Soonoo's seven and in between us was Dayanand. There were in all eight participants but I was scared of only Dayanand. The whistle went on and all the eight of us were ready for the departure. Then the white flag in Motee's hand came down and all the sixteen eager feet grabbed the advantage. Dayanand and Soonoo both being more alert than me were steps away from me. This distance were maintained up to the last pole near Kalimaye where Gowtam in the midst of the road was waving a red flag. The first to overtake him was Dayanand followed by Soonoo and I was the third. I increased my speed. I had to cross my sister once again in front of our house where I saw him while coming. I had two hundred metres to go; my sister was almost at the same distance. I decided to overtake Soonoo within the next twenty-five metres and before crossing my sister and touching the arrival line I left Dayanand behind me. But what happened next was out of my imagination. We were hardly crossing the house of Bharat Mahton when Soonoo with a fast speed overtook Dayanand. I too increased my speed and, before coming to Dadibal's house near the huge Longan tree, was successful in overtaking Dayanand.

I plucked more courage but. . .

Facing the speed of Soonoo I was at the same time bewildered and demoralized and yet I refused to give up. Approaching our house and coming by my sister I was capable of joining Soonoo but I didn't have enough stamina left in my feet to overtake him. I wanted to slow down my speed I was hardly at fifty metres from the arrival line — the win — and the five rupees . . . and the toy — the tank . . . There was no other means left to win than . . . so I let my left foot strike at Soonoo's left foot and the time he took to control himself after the stumbling managed to leave him two steps behind. And the rest came automatically and when I crossed arrival line Soonoo was some five to six metres away from me. I was declared the winner and was hailed by my friends but I wasn't able to look squarely in the face of Soonoo. After the final race every winner was awarded. With the five rupee note I went straight to Soonoo and holding his both hands I entrusted him the win. He looked at me and before he would have said anything to me I left him.

It was the next day. I was in the backyard with a couple of my friends picking prunes from the heavily laden tree when my sister came to me and gave me something which after holding in my hand I looked at in amazement. When I asked my sister where did she get it she said:

"Soonoo was in a hurry. He just asked me to give it to you."

The object in my hand was the key-winding tank at Michel's shop I was longing for.

Visa for Cinema

The Anand Cinema Hall of Triolet was recently built. My craziness for films was initiated by those friends of mine who were employees in the sugar estate. They used to speak of every new film, seen by them, in such promposity that I became impatient to see them. They were my elders and had the means of going to the movie at least once per week. Some of them were in the habit of doing it twice. I was among those few boys of the locality who were students and did not have money in pocket for ticket like those young labourers. But like them I also very eagerly would wait for every new film poster. The posters were in French which I was asked to read for them from the first to the last word. But our greatest expectation was for the posters of the Sunday matinee show which were stuck on the wall of the nearby shop on Friday morning. He who happened to be the first to see them would go on publicizing them amongst others. Those were the days of Nadia, Bhagwan, Baboorao, Tyrone Power and Errol Flynn. We were all great fans of their fighting stunts.

The courtyard in front of our house was not a large one and yet along with that of the neighbour it became expanded. Wall between two houses was not a common thing in those days, so the two combined yards automatically had become the playground of all the children living in the vicinity of Kalimaye, that is our region. The games played by us were football, "Cassee-Cote", *Kabaddi*, hide-and-seek, but the most popular of them all was the marble games and particularly the "Triangle". Our front yard was littered with stones, an obstacle which never stopped children gathering in dozens. They would call it their playground.

Saturday and Sunday being two school holidays were the days when children, even from long distances, came to join us in the open competition. We had to go in different groups and choose separate areas to play our different games. There were two specific areas for the most popular marbles game with money as bet. The aim of the money stake was almost the same for all the children and that was to win at least fifteen cents for the Sunday matinee show. The able players had chances to win but then with better luck novice player like me also had his share of chance.

To begin the "Triangle" game one of the players had to draw a triangle on the ground and a limit line at fifteen to twenty feet away. Two to seven players were allowed to play in each group and every player had to have a marble in his hand as a striker. Each of them had to put his coin in the drawn triangle for participation and was entitled to play two games for every single cent. The game would start by throwing the strikers one by one to the limit line. The right of playing first came to the player whose marble was found nearest to the line. From there the striker was thrown back to the triangle. In case a coin in the triangle was struck by the marble of a player he got temporary possession on the coin until his striker got struck by another player's marble. Whoever succeeded in eliminating more players became the best winner. It took several games and several hours to win the cost of the so cherished cinema ticket.

In those days the cost of a third class ticket was 30 cents and children had to pay only half the cost. But even these fifteen cents were not easy to acquire. In order to participate in the game a minimum of one cent was required for which some of us had to fight a crusade. On every Saturday evening I went, with couple of friends, to the already harvested canefields of the nearby estate to collect dry cane stumps. Those old stumps, after being uprooted for fresh plantation, were left on the demarcation stone walls. We had to shake and knock up the soil from the old stump roots before putting them in our gunny bag. These stumps we used as fuel for our cooking purposes. My mother gave me two cents weekly for each bag. This two cents coin provided for me four chances to win a ticket. The winning was very blissful to me because it only came after losing several times.

The betting was done without the knowledge of my parents. The day my father came to know about it he tried to put a stop to it by not allowing us to play the marble game. Despite the warning of my father we managed to continue with so many tricks of our own. One of them was not to display the coins in the triangle. One of the players would keep all the betting coins in his pocket and in their place we

Slices from a Life

would have in the triangle a few capsules, caps of lemonade bottles.

The first day I was able to win twenty cents on my own the Anand Cinema had programmed "*Bhoot Bungla*", a film by Bhagwan Baboorao. There was another film along with it but my friends and I were mad after our two favourite comperes who with their iron fists used to give a very hard time to the villains.

The matinee shows were always scheduled for one o'clock in the afternoon. In our eagerness and thrilling mood for cinema we did not care to take our lunch and tried our best to leave for Anand by 12.30 and sometimes much earlier in order to secure good seats. We had to walk more than one kilometre for it. Our group, aged between eleven and seventeen, was of ten to fifteen. The big boy incharge to push himself in the rushing crowd by the booking window to buy our tickets was always Soneet, the most agile of the group.

The losers in the Triangle game were not always left behind. One or two of them would accompany us without a single cent in pocket. In situations like this Dayanand and Soonoo would come forward with their usual craftiness to bluff the short-sighted entrance keeper with tickets of earlier shows picked by some of us. The other way to give easy access to the "without tickets" was to force in such a hustle and bustle that those having no ticket were sent inside without being seen by the keeper. It was the "grand époque" of the cinema. We manifested our joy inside the cinema hall without caring about the objection of other spectators or the management. Our going to cinema was not only to listen but to see. At the starting of every fighting scene we would start clapping our hands, hailing and encouraging the heroes to finish with the cruel villain for once and all. The elder would not approve this sort of disturbances and we were, on many occasions, reprimanded by the management. But the fact the elders were not able to understand was so simple. It was our way of enjoying and sharing those stunt films. Enjoyment in silence could not have been a complete one.

The Film Without an 'End'

Whenever I come to think of my student days I am mostly reminded of its dullness. When I was in the primary level the days used to be insipid and sluggish. I have never been a brilliant figure and in those days I was much more indolent. Those were days of natural circumstances and situations and for that very reason they were not as painful as those of my college days, hardly of two years. And yet during that small period I lost a very important part of my life to no purpose. I watched those moments in vain going away with a flashy speed.

My parents, especially my mother, had to fight tooth and nail in sending me to college. In the very outset I was eager to become someone in order to make mother's dream realized. But in the glamour of the town's life and by the influence of the ways of my classfellows my determination dashed to pieces with time. The desire of well dressing, well eating like my friends and to look smart to the girls around started bubbling in me. I went on forgetting that my mother had to thrive in the canefield and at the same time breed cow to keep my study go on. I got ashamed to carry on my shoulder the shabby canvas bag made by the village cobbler for my college books. I made continuous request to my mother for a better looking bag. I would say:

"I'll stop going to college if I am not given a decent bag."

Similarly, I began harassing my parents for better clothes and shoes. I didn't have the whole set of books like my other classmates. Bringing the issue to my mother and telling her of the daily scolding by the teachers I would start giggling like a child in front of her. My sister Tiffi would come forward and try to explain to me that it wasn't fair to be so imposing. She promised me, on behalf of my mother, that I'll be getting everything with time. She knew it as well that things were not as easy. Mother had also to pay off the debt from her income after completing the needs of others in the house. I knew of the fact that my bus fare was in itself a burden to my mother yet she managed to find it for me. Being not successful by one means or the other she would sell the eggs kept apart for more difficult moments.

Disappointed with the unfulfilled everyday demands of mine I opted to neglect my study. The little hotel where my friends used to go for their lunch was not too far from Neo College and was known as Hotel Luxor. My friends had already talked a lot about its cookies such as *Hhajia* and *Nimki*, that is, the gateaux piment. Its Alouda also was much praised. I used to take my lunch with the cookies of the Tamil auntie sitting by the college whom we, all the students, called Attey. After being tempted by the praise of Hotel Luxor's cookies I joined the group of Chand who was one of my few best friends in the college. I started going around with them and let myself give up the habit of eating Attey's stuff. I couldn't afford to eat at Hotel Luxor but then an idea came to me. I was living at my sister Sossil's place in Maupin Street in school days. I returned to the village only on Fridays to come back to town on Mondays. So in the weekends I went around my village friends and collected mangoes. Fruit Citère, sugarcane, tamarind and other fruits were not easily available in Port Louis. I took them straight to college on Mondays. The friends amongst whom I distributed the fruits were to pay for my Hotel Luxor's bills, in turns.

The day I escape from school at midday to go for a matinee show of *Kali Ghata* at the old Luna Park my ticket was equally paid by my friends. I was caught in the cinema hall by Bhim, an elder of our neighbourhood. It was a Thursday and I had to return home on the next day. When Friday came I found the fear in me increasing. I was scared by the idea that Bhim might have reported my going to cinema instead of being at the college to my parents. But I was more worried with the thought of my mother's pain caused by my deed than my getting battered. When I reached village on Friday my mother had gone for fodder. It was only when she came back, kissed me on both cheeks and talked to me in the usual way that I got relieved of all the worries. I had to thank Bhim inwardly for having spared me.

The misbehaviour continued and once every week I ran away from school to matinee shows. But as it happens that hundred days for the thief and one day for the policeman, our ugly trick was brought to the knowledge of our principal

Mr. Nepal. One Thursday along with four other friends I was watching the Hindi film '*Sindbad the Sailor*' in the third class of the Majestic Cinema when suddenly two men with a torch came by us. The light of the torch was thrown on our faces and before we got an idea of what was happening a slashing of *rotin bazaar* on our backs started. We were used to the taste of that rod, so it didn't take us much time to know of what was taking place. With the help of the other teacher of our college Mr Nepal dragged us from the cinema hall. In those days the third class seats of Majestic were located on the top. The stairs of which were so narrow that while being dragged I had my knee wounded. Without paying any heed to our imploration the two teachers pushed the five of us inside the old little 'Austin-Ten' and we were taken straight to our college in La rue Madame. There was of more shame in the thrashing of that day than pain because the punishment took place in the presence of the girls from other section.

Of Death

I have already written, in "Slices from a Life", about the feeling of death which I had when my sister "Tiffi" was dying in my arms. Death is a mystery as well as a revealer. To some of our philosophers it is the only truth of life, to others it is not an end but the beginning. Rajneesh epitaph declared it as "Never born never died just left one planet to another one."

Before I come to the story of my niece's death I want to mention an incident that took place only a few days back. A relative of mine who had completely lost his power of vision because of diabetes was on his death bed. He was given his last drops of *Ganga jal* by his kins and there was a recital of *Hanuman Chalisa* going on to make his departure less painful when suddenly the dying man looked from left to right. He asked his daughter and son to come close to him. He said:

"I can see you. Come to me. I can see everybody in the room."

Holding the hands of his two children he looked at them with a very live smile and then to his wife. And retaining his smile he closed his eyes for ever. This unexpected way in which he had his sight back at the very last moment speaks by itself of death. Whatever be the medical explanation.

The death of my eldest sister's daughter is another question unanswered. Despite explanations given, death the revealer seems not to reveal everything. My niece's name was Rajkumari. She was the most loved girl in the area because of her loveliness and manners. She was in her teenage when the polio epidemic had taken the country by storm. Children under eighteen weren't allowed to travel by any means of transport. The "polio enfantine" was raging and making victims by numbers. I was of ten to eleven years at that time—that is one year younger than Rajkumari. One day she suddenly started suffering from an undiagnosed disease.

My parents did their might and main to give her all

possible treatment but as children were not allowed to travel by any means of transport we had to rely on home treatment alone. Though Rajkumari wasn't a victim of the polio threat she wasn't able to get down from her bed even with all her limbs unaffected. Doctors came and went but her conditions remained the same. One strange thing about her disease was that in spite of her physical weakness she had the stamina sustained and her voice was all the time as vibrant and full of merriment. Rajkumari had an unusual habit of bearing a red *Tika* on her forehead, a permission not granted to unmarried girls. She would not listen to anybody advising her to wear a black *Tika* instead. Perhaps it was the only issue to which Rajkumari did never obey. She was so liked by everyone that the people's objection to her red *Tika* had to get dropped.

She remained cheerful up to her last day. As always she was bathed and put on clean clothes. Her condition had started deteriorating from a few days back subject to which relatives and neighbours were always on visit. It was because of the attending crowd that my sister forgot to put her usual red *Tika* on her forehead. From a night before I was hearing from the elders that her time has come and she would be leaving us at any time. She had told my mother and sister on the previous night that she had already watched her last sunset.

From the early morning, after observing the death symptoms, the elders were gathered around her bed. All of a sudden, my mother and sister started crying. Rajkumari was dead. Death with smile and peace on her face. Weeping and wailing continued for a long time after which the body of Rajkumari was given a bath and clothed in white. A black *Tika* was marked on her forehead. The body was surrounded with petals and an earthen lamp lighted by its head.

It was perhaps a full hour after her death that mourners who were close to the body observed something strange. Rajkumari's pupils were blinking. Everybody was taken aback and the astonishment was bigger when Rajkumari's eyes opened widely and a smile flickered on her lips. People from outside rushed in and it was amidst a sort of tumult that we were able to hear Rajkumari's voice:

"You put a wrong *Tika* on my forehead. I'm back for my red one. Don't lose time."

My sister started screaming. My mother consoled her and asked to bring quickly the red *Tika*. Rajkumari was in life and everybody was in a dead silence. The red *Tika* was brought by someone and my sister, after wiping the dark one, put the red *Tika* on the recomer's forehead. She smiled and cast a glance around and with eyes stopped at her mother said:

"Now I am going. It's a very long journey. I can't wait longer."

She started closing her eyes slowly and with joining fingers uttered her last words:

"Do excuse me for all wrongs done. *Pranam.*"

And this time it was the real death. The greatest truth and yet the unknown. The rest is up to the science to reveal. But one thing is crystal clear. The day when there will be no death there will be no life at all because the ultimate truth is death. But alas the child too dies.

In the words of Longfellow:
"There is a reaper whose name is Death
And, with his sickle keen,
He reaps the bearded grain at a breath
And the flowers that grow between."

There are of course instances when man doesn't live at all. And we know it also that man starts dying drop by drop from the very second of his birth and that is why death is great.

The Hot Groundnut

The shop from where we used to buy foodstuffs wasn't far from our house. It was known to us by the name of "La Boutique Michèle". The names of the old shopkeeper's children were also Christian names and yet on the wooden plank above the interior door there were pictures of Chinese deities. In front of these pictures incense sticks were lighted every morning. All the three nameplates over the three doors of the shop were in Chinese revealing nothing to the village folks. It was known as La Boutique Michele only to those well acquainted with the area. The building of wood and corrugated iron belonged to Sookhdeo Gopaul and it was on rent since long. Behind the shop were the houses of the Gopaul family. Sookhdeo had a vegetables stall in the veranda of the shop. Before becoming his customer my parents used to buy their vegetables from Sadhoo Beedassy, another vendor coming from Trios Boutiques, who went door to door with his hand-pulled wooden cart. But when Sookhdeo *Bhaiya* started the business we shifted to him. His wife who was very intimate to my parents was my *Bhawji* according to village tradition.

Contrary to Sookhdeo *Bhaiya* who was very strict in his trade, his wife, that is my Jhoonee *Bhawji*, was very kind-hearted. Whenever my mother sent me for vegetables I preferred going behind the shop at Sookhdeo's house instead of the vegetables stall. This I did because Jhoonee *Bhawji* was there to give me guavas, patate chinois, litchees and other fruits free of cost after my routine purchase. She liked me more than all the children around and she would never call me by my name but simply Munna. And with what a tenderness! She was as sweet as charming. My age at that time was hardly of ten or eleven. At the very first sight of me she would forget every one in front of her and start talking to me always in the same stereotype way—

"How are you? What have you eaten today? Why do you look so sad? Why you didn't come yesterday?"

Slices from a Life

It seemed to me that I was a babe of four or five years in her eyes instead of my real age. Anyway I always cherished her questions. In her free time she would go on chatting with me for long. She always picked selected fruits from the various fruit trees behind the house. She kept them for me till evening and then only gave them to others if I failed to reach her house. Her son Dutt was younger than me but we soon became friends. In spite of this friendship he had to address me as uncle on his mother's advice. I was embarrassed by being called uncle by so intimate a friend and it also seemed to add more years on my head.

Sookhdeo *Bhaiya* was lovingly called "*Bartan Manjwa*" by his friends. It wasn't to tease him but to share a certain fun. It came out of an incident. A few women customers of Sookhdeo *Bhaiya* had a short of grievance that because of too many customers he had raised the prices of the vegetables. In their annoyance these women went to buy their vegetables from the Beedassy brothers to which Sookhdeo in mere frivolity said:

"You wait and see. They will return to me like the hens bound to return to the washing spot of defiled plates. Because the hens who do not get any grain after wandering the entire yard have to come back to the *Bartan Manjwa*."

It was from that very instant Sookhdeo was given the nickname by his friends. He was so jovial despite his strictness in business that he never took it a miss. His roasted groundnuts were very popular in the whole village. His method of roasting them was very unique. It wasn't the common way of roasting them in a pan of hot sands. He happened to use a long '*gamelle*' with a crank, in the middle. He had it fixed on two hooks over the fire and it was by constant turning of the messkettles that he had the nuts roasted in a very special way spreading a pleasant aroma in the air.

They were also very tasty and people flocked to buy. In those days one used to get a full fist of groundnuts for five cents. The fist measure used by Sookhdeo *Bhaiya* was very accurate. It was only on rare occasions that his fist offered nineteen or twenty-one nuts instead of the twenty. If any of our friends happened to find twenty two after the counting he would start leaping with joy and we all were bound to consider him the luckiest of us all.

I bought nuts merely on two or three occasions from the stall of Sookhdeo *Bhaiya*. I used to go straight to his house where Jhoonee *Bhawji* filled my pocket to the brim and very easily I got up to forty nuts for my five cents. Once Jhoonee *Bhawji* said to me with her usual smile:

"Your pocket is too small."

I had got only two pairs of trousers. One was patched and the second one was almost as old as the first one. When I was wearing one the other one was stretched on the rope to be dried after the wash. I got a burning desire in me to have a pair of trousers with deeper pockets so I took hold of the patched one and tore it in hiding, then went on insisting to my mother for a new one. My mother put off my demand and one day said in anger:

"You should have born in a well-off family."

To which I promptly said:

"You used to say that we were the richest in the area. How is it that today we are so poor?"

"You go and ask your father who, like Harishchandra, allowed himself to be plundered."

After her continuous scolding my mother submitted herself to my demand and one day she bought the piece of cloth and sent me to the tailor. My tailor's name was Adam Bundhoo. On seeing me with the cloth he very bluntly said that owing to the rush of approaching new year he could not make it before two weeks' time. I came back home and started whimpering in front of my mother and in a sort compelled her to accompany me to the tailor's shop. Adam *Bhai* complied with my mother's request and said:

"Nevertheless, *Chachi*, it will be ready only after one week."

My mother accepted it but to me it was as though the week was longer than a month. When my mother left the shop I said to my tailor:

"Adam *Bhai*, see to it that I get two pockets in my trousers and let it be bit more bigger."

"Do you intend to carry an elephant in your pocket?"

He wasn't agreeable in the beginning complaining that the cloth wasn't sufficient for any additional form but then he agreed. It was after a long fortnight that I presented myself to Jhoonee *Bhawji* in my new trousers. She looked at me and said with a smile:

"You will have to give me ten cents to fill these two pockets of yours."

And my pockets were filled fullbrim for only five cents. The serial continued for months. As always she had filled my pockets with nuts and kissed me on both cheeks before going back to her routine. I left the place and was coming through the side road when suddenly under the tamarind tree I met Sookhdeo *Bhaiya*. Looking at me bulky pockets he asked me:

"What do you have in them?"

"Groundnuts."

"So much?"

"I bought it from Jhoonee *Bhauji*."

"How much did you pay?"

"Five cents."

"Impossible! Your *Bhauji* cannot give you nuts worth fifty cents for five cents. How dare she push me to bankruptcy? Are you sure that she gave you al these nuts?"

"No. . . She didn't give me . . . "

"So you did it yourself? You the son of Pateesingh happened to steal?"

He forced me to empty my both pockets and with very sharp rebuke ordered me to leave the place immediately.

The Fear

My cousin Lutchmee, who had her upbringing in our family, got married. I had known my brother-in-law before the marriage and I didn't like him from the very beginning. At the time of the marriage I was hardly eight years old. I objected to the wedding and went on requesting my mother and my sister Savitri, whom we all called Tiffi, not to let my cousin marry a person of whom I was so allergic. Despite my unwillingness the wedding took place. When Lutchmee went to her in-laws' house at Cottage I lost my blissful moments of childhood. She used to love me more than anybody at home. It was she who, holding my finger, taught me to walk. I was afraid of the dark and while lulling me to sleep she chanted the "*Hanuman Chalissa*" instead of a lullaby.

I had two aunts living at Cottage. Transport in those days was scarce and we had to go to them on foot and through footways and cart tracks between the cane fields. My aunts reported to us of the cruelties inflicted to my cousin by her husband Beesoon, who was a drunkard. I was pained. Learning that my most beloved *Didi* was ill-treated even by her in-laws, who approved of her being battered. After constant hammering I succeeded to convince my father and the next day my cousin was brought back home from that butcher's place. To me it was happiness regained.

The children of the village were warned by their elders not to stay or play under banyan, tamarind and blackberry trees at midday. It was believed that they were the dwelling places of ghosts and shrews. Whenever I was scared by such thoughts, my cousin Lutchmee advised me to chant the *Hanuman Chalissa*. During the school holidays I passed most of the time playing with my friends under the huge tamarind tree, just at a stone's throw from my house, and whenever I heard the sounds of the chapel and the Shivala's bells I started murmuring the verses of the fear riddance book. Then came the days when I had to stop my studies, after only one year, at the Neo College of Port Louis, and started picking up minor jobs here and there. Having an aptitude for drawing and painting I got my first meagre payment by completing the nameplates of the first lorry in our neighbourhood owned by Bhai Motee. I did the job, hardly started by a painter who didn't turn up, for reasons unknown to me. It was under the old "Jamblon tree", where the ironsmith Bhai Gajadhur had his workshop. The two words to be written were "Georgie Transport" which I had to write on two long planks and the small nameplate at the back and all this for just twenty rupees. A couple of friends who used to be with me during the four days' work did leave me alone at the very start of the deep ringing of the church bell. I was left alone for the confrontation with the devil of the old blackberry tree which was supposed to appear at noon sharp. These stories of ghosts and shrews were seriously told to us by Mano, the fisherman, that we were bound to believe them. He went up to the saying that once a lady in dark came out of the tree and tried to strangle him. The most scared of us all was Dadibal who pretended to have seen the shrew swinging on the tree. In spite of Lutchmee's disapproval of all such stories it took me a long time to free myself of the misled.

I managed to buy brushes and paints with the earned money and continued with my hobby and part-time job of signboard painting. I started getting praise for my drawing and paintings and one day I was asked to do a couple of murals at the temple by the *Pujari*. It was a request and not an offer which I accepted and painted the pictures of Sita and Ram on one of the walls and that of Durga on another one. My real assignment came from Shri Kissonlall Chintamanee of Bambous, who while in Triolet, was my teacher at the Neuvième Mille Baithka. I stayed in Bambous for a couple of weeks to paint three pictures of the Hindu deity at the temple of the village including that of Saraswati on the front top. During my work, every morning, I saw a very changing girl coming for *Pujc*. I tried to talk to her but she never replied to any of my questions so one day I said:

"Are you mute?"

The next day, to my great surprise and regret I came to know that she was really mute. She remained in my mind for long, quite long. Let's go back to the real aspect of this down memory lane that is of fear, of ghosts and shrews. In fact, no encounter with any ghost or shrew under any tamarind and blackberry tree ever took place but still the banyan tree which happened to be our most favourite play spot where we had all sorts of games, from football to fencing *à la* Douglas Farbanks Jr and pretending to be Johnny Weismuller, the Tarzan, by swinging from the fibrous root to root of the banyan tree. On that particular day, we were playing police and thief "hide-and-seek".

A young person by the nickname of Chiranya in the vicinity had disappeared for three days. There were so many talks going on concerning his disappearance. Some said that he had a quarrel with his elder brother and had left the house for ever. The pessimist went as far as saying that he had drowned himself in the sea. The gossipmongers had it that because he had an affair with Baldewa's wife it may be that he had been killed and buried somewhere by the rival.

There were large ruins of a sugar factory all around the banyan tree, a proper place to play hide and seek. We were divided into two groups, one of police and the other of thieves' gang. The leader of the police force was Hassen and Jawahar was the chief of the thieves. The thieves were already in hiding when we, in the police group, were seeking from wall to wall and room to room with wooden guns. We were told by our spy that some of the thieves were hiding in the cane field adjacent to the ruin. We heard the whistle and all the five of the police group standing on the roofless walls went on swinging from the banyan roots and landing in the midst of the ready-for-harvest green cane field. I was behind Hassen. Our first arrest was Gaffoor who hadn't got enough time to cover himself completely with straws. Putting him out of the game, Hassen and I moved to the direction from where came the noise of the rustling of leaves. Not too far from us stood a mango tree whose surrounding part was plain. Both of us saw something moving beneath the tree. Without losing time, Hassen jumped like a hound and took hold of the object which was swinging on a branch. Before Hassen could identify his catch, I was horrified to see a dead body in his arms. It gave me the creeps, and my friend having discovered his holding was stunned with eyes wide open. Both of us took to our heels.

We did the police job by finding out the dead body of the missing Chiranya. I had never known of fear to such a degree. It was worse with Hassen. He looked as though he was

Slices from a Life

unconscious. Gaffour and Vidyanand took him to his house. At night, when my friends came to see me, I was surrounded by my parents and chanting the *Hanuman Chalissa* to overcome the horror which seemed to have frozen inside me. My friends told me of Hassen's terror. Even the priest of the temple had much difficulty in separating him from the wooden pillar of his house, he was so tightly clung with. Chingroo Ojha was still struggling to free him from the ghost of Chiranya with his hocus-pocus. For more than a week, I carried in my mind, everywhere I went, that horrific scene and its smell. The mango tree was added to the list of dreary tamarind, blackberry and the banyan trees. After a horrible week, I joined my friends under the banyan tree but for Hassen if was a fear at its most terrific form.

Back to the Cane Field

I had to give up my study and start working as from the age of fourteen. In spite of it I wasn't able to acquire a permanent job and for which I was from time to time scolded by my parent. I went beating the air from place to place but in vain. Prior to this I tried my best to help my parent in the dire straits by working as a hawker with basket of vegetables on my head. I worked in tobacco shop, in the sugar cane field and helped my mother in procuring fodder for the cow and the couple of goats. I also worked as an auctioneer of vegetables in the Central Market at Port Louis with a relative of mine, Mr Raj-Karun Gayan. I coudn't continue it because the journey from Triolet to Port Louis and back on bicycle lended to me by my employer was very hard for me owing to my fragile health. I had to return to the sugar cane field. My mother was much more pained than me for the hard work I had to go through. I had to run a lot to be able to have a bus receiver licence. I was introduced to the manager of Rose-Hill Bus Service through the letter of a relative of mine and was accepted as part-timer. It wasn't easy for me to reach Rose Hill (from Triolet) every morning before five. I had to report in time to be able to replace any absentee. The easy way for me was to stay at my brother's place who was then living at Arab Street in Port Louis.

I had to leave my brother's house early at four in the morning for the Victoria Station in order to catch the first bus going to Rose Hill. It was the winter period and I had to walk more than one kilometre alone through narrow streets in the chilling cold dimness. I had to walk another long kilometre in Rose Hill to reach the garage in Hugnin Street. I had a pair of khaki uniforms tailored with debt from a friend. Three long weeks went on training. In the very beginning I was given only one day in a week to replace the unattended because there were others like me in the waiting line. It was so despite my arriving earlier to the others. We were known as "Stepné" and sometimes teased as "*Serre*

Coin". The station master at the garage used to show certain favour to those arriving after me and my only chance was when I used to be the only one in the waiting line. The conductor under whom I got my coaching said to me one day:

"You will never get more than one day per week."

"Why?"

"You have to grease the Chef de Gare's palm. *Bizin trempe la gorge.*"

Bribe him would have meant depriving myself either of my return ticket or my day's meal which was bread and gateaux-piment. But then I was bound to do it and from that day I started to have two days per week instead of the only one. But I had to present on spot all the seven days of the week. One day on my home back for three consecutive days my sister-in-law said to me:

"*Pooja sé bhari dandwat,*" meaning that the going and coming was much harder a nut to crack than the work itself.

It was indeed very painful for me to come back four or five days without work but my mother would console me by saying:

"Do not lose patience. The fruit of fortitude is always sweet. The income of these two days is better than nothing at all."

Whenever I started a new job it was with the firm idea that whatsoever I'm doing will not be for ever. So let me do it and endure it until I get a job of my liking. I had a great desire to become a teacher, a wish which was impossible because I didn't have any required qualification. I had to stop my study at the Neo College only after one and a half years because of the lack of means. I opted for the bus job with the same idea and wanted to carry on with at least for a whole year so that I could have some money to continue my study but it didn't happen. It was perhaps just two months that the undesired event took place prior to which the first one I'm going to speak of was the prelude.

It was early morning. Three or four passengers entered the bus I was working in at Ambrose. The bus was almost full. Two of them managed to have their seats in the first row. I was issuing tickets at the extreme rear. Being still a beginner I didn't have that equilibrium and speed. The bus reached Grand River and when it stopped at a bus stop a passenger came in followed by a ticket examiner. Standing in front of the first seats he requested the two passengers for their tickets for the punching. I hadn't yet reached the two passengers of the first row to collect their fare and for that reason they didn't have any ticket yet. The ticket examiner asked them the place where they boarded and when they said it to be Ambrose the inspector fished out the report book. After jotting down a few lines he asked me to sign beneath, which I did. Three days later I had to report myself to the manager of the bus service. I appeared before Mr Goburdhun, the Manager, who a few weeks back had provided the opportunity of my joining the company. He very attentively listened to my clarification of the problem. He then asked me about my interrupted education and my parent. When I told him the name of my father he looked at me for a while and said:

"All right this being your first mistake you are only being warned not to make it again."

I had an air of relief my job was safe and as from next day I went to work with more confidence. Unfortunately as my mother had to stay a few weeks later the job wasn't meant for me. Some three weeks after my resuming, a man walking with the help of crutch accompanied by a little girl boarded the bus at the Maingard bus stop in Beau Bassin. A person sitting on the first seat shifted to the back to allow him the place. The little girl got a seat behind the lame person. I approached the newcomer for the fare and he just gave a sign to collect the fare from the little girl. I went to the girl who was of the age of six or seven. She handed me a twenty five cent coin. When I asked her the destination she said:

"La gare Port Louis."

It was the terminus and the fare from Beau Bassin to that place was twenty five cents per seat. The little girl was entitled to half the fare so the tended fare being inadequate I told her:

"This is for one person, what about yours?"

"It is included," she replied.

"How is it? One person's fare is twenty-five cents, yours is fifteen, which makes it forty cents."

The lame man in front of her, supposed to be her father, riposted:

"We are travelling for years and have always been paying

Slices from a Life 99

the same sum."

There was an old woman sitting by the girl who said to me slowly:

"My son! They beg near the Central Market. Do not ask them for more. They may not have it."

I took hold of the twenty-five cents extended by the girl and issued two tickets—one of fifteen cents and other of ten. I took it easy with the very thought that let it be in their favour.

But the coincidence wanted it otherwise. It was once again at Grand River that I had the ticket examiner entering the bus after a passenger. After checking the first row he came to the girl. He took her two tickets, looked at them and then asked me very quietly:

"What is the fare from Beau Bassin to Port Louis?"

Without waiting any reply from me he took out his report book. Three days later I was summoned to appear before the Manager. And on that day, with the billhook in my hand I was back in sugar cane field where the harvest was at its culminating point.

The Day I Left the Cane Fields

My father was at times very hot-tempered and at times very kind-hearted. I hardly had his kind-heartedness but his temperament of prompt anger I have it almost the same way. So if at a very young age I did join the sugar cane fields it was with full of enthusiasm and joy but when after a short period I was compelled to leave it, if was because of that very hot temperament of mine. I had to discontinue my study just after two years at the secondary level and had to wander and suffer kicks while looking for a job in those days of dire straits. My mother, who nourished the dream of seeing me in a white-collar job was against my joining the cane fields. From my very childhood I had bronchial problems owing to which my health was always fragile. Despite my feeble body I had in me very high spirits for the cutting and loading of sugar canes—an aspiration considered to be a folly by my mother. She used to go on reminding me that it was cane fields with the burning sun over the head. Because of this constant unwillingness of my mother I had to try my hands at different jobs one after another. From some places I had to move and from others I was chucked out.

At last, in spite or my mother's withholding, I succeeded in making my entrance in the canefields. Dado Bhowji, our neighbour who in days of droughts was in the habit of organising the "*Harparowri*", an imploration ceremony for rain, was my rescuer. After a fifteen days' *puja* in the honour of Lord Indra, god of rain, the ritual of sowing paddy in a field of the sugar estate was performed by the women of the locality. And by chance after the second or third day of the completion of the singing ceremony, it started raining. The estate owners very happily came forward to congratulate Dado Bhowji, the leading figure of the "*Harparowri*". And it was through Dado Bhowji, who was much respected by the proprietors of the sugar estate, that I got my job with a pay of sixty cents per day. In the beginning I was allotted the job of weeding in the fields, then came the manuring and "*glanner*", that is the collecting of leftover canes. Some three months later I joined the "second *bande*", the better paid labourers for the cutting and loading of the sugar canes.

The overseers of the estate were very severe but it was one of the three owners of whom the workers were the most scared. The one who was slim and good-looking had in him some kindness. He wasn't in the habit of using abusive language vis-a-vis the labourers but the other two particularly the obese one with his double chin could not start any reproach without calling names and abusive terms. The news of his arrival in the working sites instantly provoked alertness in the workers and their speed of work was to change into that of a machine.

On that specific day I was working in a field opposite the cremation ground. It was the most stony field of the estate and the cutting of canes was really very difficult because the space between the two demarcation walls of stones was much narrow. The year being without drought the production was good and the canes were dense. Because of the density the cutting had become more difficult. The first grade labourers with their dexterity in the job were able to complete their work and return home before midday. We of the second group comprising younger ones and women had to work longer to complete our allotment. The strong outburst of the midday sun. No leaf was moving. I was left behind by my colleagues in that suffocating heat. Time as though had come to a stop. My clothes drenched with sweat were stuck to my body. The coolness of the sweat was boosting up my morale to complete the work despite the tiredness and the uneasiness amidst the heat. After the departure of the first grade labourers the number of women collecting green cane leaves as fodder for their cows was limited. There was no patch of cloud in the sky that could have provided us with little shade for even a moment.

A few minutes before my left side friend Taleb had informed me of the "Captain's" arrival. The fat double chin owner was known as "Captain" to all the labourers and he seemed pleased by the nickname. I straightened my body to have a glance at the standing canes from which the green leaves were already chopped out by Dado Bhowji. She had three cows in her stable and for that very reason after collecting fodder from his son Bhim's share she had to have it from my side too. There was still a length of forty-fifty feet of canes in the line in front of me. Being aware of my lagging I tried my utmost to increase my speed in order to join my friends. I gave the billhook in my hand more active motion. In that hasty process a few canes were bound to cut off above the required height from the roots. That was the moment when the "Captain" coming from my back started yelling. He vociferated:

"You bastard! Is it the way to cut the canes? How could it grow again if cut so up?"

I said nothing. He came nearer and used abusive language towards my mother and sister.

"These three to four inches of canes over the roots you are leaving them for whom? Your father or your brother-in-law?"

I stopped my work for a moment and looked at the obese man standing by me. In a very slow voice I said:

"As from now this will not happen."

"But you scoundrel, who is going to pay for the damage already done? Am I your brother-in-law?"

"Please do not use abusive terms."

"You son of a bitch, you afford to give me order?"

The heat was unbearable. Abuses added to it, it became intolerable. But we the labourers had to get accustomed to it. The bill hook in my right hand was suddenly sparkled by the rays of the sun. I said very humbly:

"I'm accepting my fault. Please do not abuse my parents."

"You order me not to abuse? Bastard! you are putting my plantation to ruin. Do you think that this estate belongs to *mari* to *mama*?"

In the meantime the shining billhook in my hand went up and with all my force I threw it in the fat man's direction. He managed to move his neck very quickly. Having missed him by inches my billhook fell down on a heap of canes. The "Captain" remained spellbound and by the time he would have opened his mouth for another abusive word, I crossed the stone walls and was out of the field.

It was my last day in the cane field. And that is not all. I didn't go back to that estate even to collect my week's salary.

When I Was Lured to Steal

I am hardly attracted by gems surely because I have never been able to know their value or else it has been a matter of '*le raisin amer*'. Thing which has been, all the time, more valuable to me than stones is a good book and I am still tempted to have in my possession all the masterpieces of literature. I was of eight or nine years when for the first time this consciousness for the preciousness of books aroused in me. And if today I derive great pleasure in not just having books around me but also in presenting them to benevolent institutions, it is in the same context and perspective of offering something as valuable as the gem. But there is one more reason attached to this regular process and that is a feeling of a certain atonement. An action to atone for something wrong done by me when I was a child of eight or nine.

My father had at that time, not too far from our house, a small tabagie. It was a banal enterprise with meagre income referring to which my mother would say:

"To depend on it means to keep my children without food."

In fact the income of the tobacco shop was not so inadequate. The reality behind the thin profit was that my father did not have enough guts to ask his customers to settle their previous account before imploring for further credit.

There were two flamboyant trees on the other side of the road opposite our shop. In summer the ground was carpeted with red petals falling from the two trees. Their branches above were as though full of blazing embers with the rays of the bright sun floating in the crimson flowers and yet beneath them the expanding shade provided a relaxing coolness. There were a few huge rocks under those trees on which the elders of the vicinity came to sit for hours and listen to the news, from the three combined newspapers—*Advance, Le Cernéen, Le Mauricien*—read and explained by my father.

When my father happened to be reading the papers I

was supposed to be in the shop attending to the customers.

In those days vehicles on the road were rare and traffic frequency very slow, sometimes at the interval of more than half an hour. So I was not scared of crossing the road from time to time enabling me to listening of the news and the attending of customers.

On that day and at that unforgettable moment I was sitting by my father who was informing the village folk, gathered around him, of the latest events of the war. I was listening with deep interest to both his reading in French and rendering in Bhojpuri when a hawker with a big bundle on his head came in the midst. He was not an unknown person to us because at the end of every month he came to our village to sell Hindi books. After spreading a cotton sheet on the ground covered with petals of flamboyant he untied his bundle and displayed the new books by scattering them to the full sheet. My father besides being his unfailing customer was also his promoter. He would be the first to buy and recommend to others those books of history and religion which he had already gone through. Even the unwilling persons were in a sort compelled to buy at least the little and the cheapest ones.

The book chosen by my father on that occasion was entitled '*Bharat Ka Itihas*', the history of India by someone with a pseudonym of '*Itihas Premi*'. Of course this fact was known to me much later. The book was a voluminous one, priced at two rupees fifty cents. After having paid the price my father handed the grey covered book to me. In the meantime some more people were gathered all around the displayed books. My father, a voracious reader, had started turning the pages of another bulky book. Others were involved either in looking at illustrations or casting a glance at the contents of books picked by them. In almost the same way I also took hold of a fully illustrated story book for children and started looking at the pictures inside. It was indeed a very attractive booklet and I was lured by it. I asked my father to buy it for me but he in his usual style said to me:

"Next time".

People around were busy looking at the books and inquiring about their prices. The story book was still in my hand and with a pretext of going through it I cast a side glance at the hawker and other persons around. Before being spotted by anybody I half opened the big history book and slided the children booklet inside it. I remained there with the big book pressed to my chest and with fear inside waited for the appropriate moment. A few minutes later the bookseller collected the remaining books from the cotton sheet and started making the bundle. It was the moment I was waiting for with all eagerness, I made a couple of steps back and ran to our house with the history book bought by my father inside which was safely hidden the booklet shoplifted by me. I was very happy. It was not a happiness of having succeeded to steal the book which my father refused to buy for me but it was the joy of possessing a gem.

The joy didn't last for long. It was at night after dinner that the children book was spotted by my father. Holding the booklet with his left hand my father, with his right hand, took hold of my wrist and bringing me close to him said in anger:

"You stole the book!"

Putting the book aside and grasping me by my arm he shook me and slapped me on both cheeks. I started crying, more by fear than pain. My mother leaving the kitchen came in. My father with another terrible slap on my face shouted:

"He has started stealing this affectionate one of yours."

It was much later that my mother, taking me in her embrace, said to me:

"You should never steal again. A child who steals books never passes his examinations."

Perhaps that might have been the cause of my not being really successful in exams and of not possessing any valid educational certificate. Anyway... I have to go on giving books in gift and continue writing — I don't know how many books, because of that one book, I cannot say what happened to that story book but the history book is still in my personal library as a great witness of time.

Lust for Books

The first book in Hindi I came across was Sharat Babu's novel "*Shesh Prashna*". It was the book which, after going through, produced in me lust for novels. My knowledge of Hindi was as limited as those of English and French. The few English and French books which I had read prior to Sharat Babu's novel were "*The Tempest*", "*Oliver Twist*", "*Les Miserables*" and "*Le Comte de Monte Christo*" in simplified editions. But the influence left upon my mind by "*Shesh Prashna*" was greater than those left by the books in English and French. Since then my yearning for books in Hindi was very much like the thirst provoked in the sugar cane field by the mid-day sun.

In our house my three sisters were as voracious readers as my mother and father. My father, despite his habit of buying, was also used to borrow books from friends. Almost all the books on the shelf were rather those dealing with religion or history but the books brought by my father from his friends were usually novels. My sisters were not allowed to read novels and yet they did read them in hiding. In imitation of which I also avoiding the sight of my father finished "*Shesh Prashna*" in a matter of two days. After that the second novel that came to my hand was "*Chandrakanta*", the bulky novel of Devkinandan Khatri. I read it in hardly four or five sittings. It was really an unputdownable, increasing in me the desire for novels to the extreme.

My father was considered, in those days, as someone with a sound knowledge of English and French but his love for Hindi was above all. He used to talk for hours on the *Ramayan*, the *Mahabharat*, and of the great heroes of history and people in the vicinity were never tired of listening to him. My mother was able to read only Hindi books. My sisters had not learnt the language in any Hindi school. From letters to words and from words to the chanting and reading of the scriptures and the "*Alha Khand*" they had got it from my mother. In spite of her being so devoted to Hindi, my mother was not in favour of my attachment to it. She would go on advising me to concentrate in the languages that could provide a job in government. Whenever she caught me reading a Hindi book she scolded me with relentless words.

At night when she found me reading a Hindi book in the light of the Kerosene lamp she would say with bitterness that I was making our difficult days more difficult by wasting the kerosene oil for nothing. When she found herself unable to stop my reading of Hindi books, the only alternative she had before her was to lock all those books in the cupboard. During the day I had to work in the sugarcane fields that is why the only time available for reading was at night. With the deprivation of books I had to struggle long for sleep. I had to wake up by four in the morning to reach the field at six sharp. In such situation it was a must for me to go to bed earlier but without reading a few chapters it was difficult to do so. The only alternative I was able to find out was to involve myself in drawing. But even then it took me hours before I could feel my eyes heavy with sleep. My mother would not spare me even for this drawing business.

It was nothing but a loss of time according to her.

Unlike my mother, my sisters were very fond of my drawing. Because of me, my sisters also were deprived of the new books brought or bought by my father. I had not yet completed "Nirmala" the novel of Premchand when my mother had snatched it from me and locked it. My weekly earning at that time was of five rupees to five fifty. When I had just started working it was only three rupees per week. On every Saturday, when I handed the money to my mother she gave me a piece of twenty five cents out of it. When she used to be in good mood she gave me an additional piece but it happened to be only once a month. My mother was ever conscious of the period. With all the burning desire I was not in a position to save money in order to buy books as I did in the time of my addiction for comics.

Sometimes, while walking along the canefields, I would let my imagination to wander to such an extent that I happened to think of a fairy a genie from the magic lamp to appear before me. Expecting them to ask me my wish and to which I would have said — please let me have around me as many books as possible. When I got bored I even felt the desire of restarting the reading of comics but those magazines in English and French of my school days never came back

Slices from a Life

from my friends who borrowed them.

My father had once again started the tobacco shop business. This time the shop was opposite our house. A small building rented to us by Samlall, the blacksmith. On some occasions my father had to take me to Port Louis along with him to purchase goods for the shop. On that memorable day, my father, after having purchased all the goods, took me to the central market where we had our tea. After the tea we went to the Nalanda Bookshop. This small bookshop was at that time in the eastern corner of the vegetables market at the end of the spices stalls. The displayed Hindi books provoked my greed and I wished all the books to become mine. During the time my father was looking for the book of his choice, I had my eyes fixed on a book in grey cover with illustration of a horseman. It was entitled "Toofan", The Cyclone. . . Temptation forced me to hold it in my hands. I turned a few pages. It was a collection of short stories by world masters. My father in the meantime, has already chosen his book. It was a book on Chhatrapati Shivaji, history's first guerilla fighter. I wished it much that my father buys the book in my hand for me. In vain. I had to place it on the rack.

It was indeed difficult for me to forget about the book even after our return home. I had noticed its price written on the right corner of the second page by the shopkeeper- seventy cents. Some two months later I had again to accompany my father to Port-Louis. This time I had in my pocket the sum of seventy cents. I had acquired a special income of one rupee and twenty five cents for the loading of sugarcanes which I did not give to my mother. Having forgotten a few items, my father asked me to wait in the market's teashop and went to complete his shopping. It was the right moment for me to go to the nearby bookshop. The chance I was thinking of almost a whole night had come by itself. I entered the bookshop. The copy of "*Toofan*" was still in the same place where I had left it. I fished out the three nickels from my pocket and gave them to the shopkeeper and suddenly I was the possessor of the great collection of world's stories. I was back to the teashop before the arrival of my father and had already concealed my treasure in the bag of goods.

The first book bought by the money of my labour is still in my personal library which has inside it the gems of Pushkin, Chekhov, Galsworthy, Benet, Munro and others.

The Rehearsal

It's an event of the days when people travelled long distances to attend the sermons of Professor Basdeo Bissoondoyal. I wasn't able to understand all that were said by Panditji during the sermons but the thing by which I was really enthralled was the personality of the professor. The other thing by which I was much attracted was the recitals by children in between the religious discourses. I started envying those children and got desirous to be equally in front of the mike and get the applause of the public. My retaining power was never as good as those of my friends of the Baitka but when the occasion came I managed to learn by heart the part allotted to me. It was a passage of two minutes entitled "The Banishment of Ram" from our textbook. I took ten days to memorise it. My teacher at the Maheswurnath Hindi Pathsala, Shri Kissoonlal, was much impressed by my reciting demeanour. Instead of letting me present it in our village function he programmed it for a sermon being held somewhere in Vacoas. It was a double challenge to me of which I was as happy as scared.

My elders at the Baitka had their uniforms of the "Swayam-Sewak". I went on requesting my parents to let me have that uniform comprising of a dark blue pants and white shirt along with a same coloured cap. But each time my request was put off by my father with the same stereotyped sentence that I was too young to join the volunteers. The afternoon I had to go to Panditji's sermon at some place in Vacoas my father was suddenly taken ill and I was put to the care of my Guruji, Kissoonlal. The little lorry put at our disposal was an old one with Bhai Bore as driver. It was packed to full with twenty persons including five children. Being the youngest of them all I was given to occupy the wooden bench in the first row. In spite of the rumbling sound of the old engine our chorus was capable of attracting the attention of the wayfarers throughout.

I became very impatient. I was going to be by the Panditji

and in front of the mike for the first time. Everybody on the lorry was immersed in the chanting and I was involved in the silent cramming of my passage. When our lorry reached the crossroads of Terre Rouge it had to stop in order to turn to the right. But once the engine was off it refused to start again. In order to help Bhai Bore some of the men got down. Half an hour of constant effort brought nothing and everybody had to come down. The lorry was pushed and brought to the next road but even the pushing didn't help the engine start. My great expectations and eagerness were turned into disappointment. Darkness started overspreading when despite a few more efforts in vain we knew that it was now impossible for us to participate in the function we thought of returning home. It had already started raining. The way back home was nearly seven miles. We had to walk in the rain. The elders tried their best to save my friends and myself from getting soaked but it wasn't easy.

From Terre Rouge to Arsenal-Tombeau the night became darker and frightening. The rain seemed not to stop at all. After having crossed the Tombeau bridge we arrived near the office of the Massillia Sugar Estate. Shri Kissoonlalji said that he knew the chief supervisor of the estate and that he had decided to stay there with the children. To those not returning home he asked them to inform their parents that they had to stay back because of the heavy rain and they would be returning home in the morning. On our calling, the door of the stone walled building was opened. We were taken inside in our soaked clothes. It was in the light of the big lamp that I recognized the field supervisor. He happened to be a close friend of my father who used to come to our place. He recognized me too and cheered me by saying:

"You, the son of Pateesingh *chacha*!" Four unexpected guests apart the four members of the family were there prior to our arrival. The playing of "*chowpar*", a dice game which was going on when we had arrived, was stopped. We were asked to change our clothes immediately and what we were provided instantly were either loose or tight trousers and shirts. I recognized the woman who handed me the clothes. She was the *Chachi* whom I had seen at our place on several occasions. In her usual intimate voice she asked me:

"How is it that you are with these people?"

Our teacher told her of everything and he also apprised

them of our way to the sermon by Panditji in which I had to participate. We were served hot milk with *paratha*. The dice game which had restarted continued for a while. In the meantime *Chachiji* had enquired about mother's health. A certain sadness on my face compelled her to take me closer and say to me:

"You are missing your mummy?"

When she didn't get any reply from me she said to my teacher:

"Why you people leave home at night with children? And how is it that you have chosen that old lorry of Bore *Bhaiya*?"

My four friends were given mats to sleep and I was taken to the opposite room to sleep on a bed already partly occupied by someone of my age.

The talking going on in the first room along with the game of dice had stopped indicating that the game was over. *Chachiji* after making me share half of the sheet of the bed sat near to me. She asked me several questions and told me of several things but when she did not find sleep in my eyes she said:

"I know why you are so sad. It is because you have not been able to recite your part. Isn't it?"

To which I lied in a low voice:

"No, *Chachi*."

"You are sad because you missed a great occasion. It's all right; come with me."

Holding my wrist she took me to the first room where my four friends were lying on the mats waiting sleep to come. Addressing those present in the room *Chachi* said:

"My little boy has something for you. Be attentive, everyone."

I was still indecisive. Everyone in the room sat upright. *Chachi* very slightly put her hand on my shoulder and smiled. It was the request to start. I plucked up courage and started reciting "The Banishment of Ram". I was afraid of missing one or two lines in the mid as in my earlier rehearsals. It didn't occur and I made it. Hands clapped and I felt a certain satisfaction though not a great pleasure.

It was three weeks later, after the great rehearsal of that night, that the Mahashivatri was celebrated in the yard of the Neuvieme Mille Maheshwarnath Pathshala. And it was then, in the midst of over five thousand people, I took the mike before Panditji started his discourse on the Mahashivratri. The applause of the public justified the rehearsal of the rainy night.

The Aroma of Grilled Maize

As he was the son-in-law of the village everybody used to call him brother-in-law or "*gharposh*", a derogative term for someone living at the cost of his in-laws. He was irritated whenever addressed as "*gharposh*" and when the children happened to tease him by this nickname he became furious. I was the only one among my friends who never addressed him by any other appellation than *bahnoyi*, meaning brother-in-law. His name was Rooplall but very few people called him by that name. As he was very slim and not well built, most of the village folks called him "Chingroo". Though he was a kind-hearted man he got easily vexed when teased. My friends and I often travelled by his oxcart while going to the seaside. When my friends started teasing him he became irritated and prevented them from taking seats on his cart. Walking behind the cart the children continued teasing him more frequently.

One day he met me on the road and gave me half-ripe lichees from his tree and said to me:

"I know that you never made fun of me; for that reason you can always travel by my cart but your friends will not be allowed."

Soonoo who was with me at that moment went to my friends and told them of Rooplall *bahnoyi's* decision. In those days Taleb was acting as the leader of the group. He threatened me:

"If you will board Chingroo's cart alone I'll drown you in the sea."

Taleb was as bad a swimmer as myself so there was no use of my getting afraid of his threat. I told my friends to do my best in order to persuade Rooplall *bahnoyi* to change his mind and allow us all to travel by his cart. It was December and the weather sultry and dry. The seaside was the only place where we were spared of the heat. Once in the water, we all stayed swimming and splashing for hours. The sun blazing above our head wasn't able to deprive us of the coolness we enjoyed in water. But reaching the seaside from where we lived was a two-kilometre journey and it wasn't easy task. In the blazing sun the road also used to be very hot and none of us was wearing "slippers" or shoes. We got sore soles due to the excessive heat. We were relieved only when we travelled by Rooplall's cart.

The next day, I reached his place a few minutes earlier. I knew the exact time he left his house. His first trip was to the factory of Solitude with the load of sugar cane. On return, he stayed for some half an hour to feed his ox and himself after which he proceeded to the seaside area from where he took his coal cargo for shops in Triolet. I waited for him to come out from his yard to the main road. When finally he came I, as usual, bid *namaste* to him and he after replying my salutation asked me to climb up on the cart. Instead of boarding I said:

"*Bahnoyi*! My friends are waiting by the chapel. Would you mind to give them seats on your cart?"

"No." He very bluntly said. "There is no place for them in my cart. Born yesterday, they talk big today. They behave with me as though they have showed me the first ray of light on my birth."

I tried much to convince him but in vain. He just went on saying that he would accept nobody on his cart except me. When I joined my friends and told them of the negative attitude of Rooplall, Soneetwa looked at me and said:

"We will have to deal with Chingroo in our own way. I presume that his maize field is close to that of yours."

The answer to the indirect question was yes, so I just nodded. My father was working as *sirdar* in Doctor Jhubboo's estate so he got half an acre of the sandy land free of cost for two years on which we planted brinjals. There were other plots around which were taken on hire basis for the same period and purpose. Rooplall had his portion of land adjacent to ours in which he had ready crops of maize and groundnut. My friends decided to visit his field, but I flatly refused to go. It was a proposal coming from Soneet and was accepted by all except me. I tried to dissuade them:

"Rooplall *bahnoyi* is a poor man."

"We are not rich people," it came from Sonalal.

After was Dadibal and that was, perhaps, because of two reasons. The first one was that he lived next to Rooplall's house and the second was his cowardliness. If he happened to be on the road and saw a policeman coming from far away he would run into his house.

Taleb, probing about, asked me a few questions and I replied. When they were told that Rooplall together with his wife and daughters always left his field at five in the afternoon so it was decided that six o'clock would be the best time to charge attack. I told them that it was difficult for me to get out of my house after five. Soneet in a mocking voice said:

"He is a girl!"

Another boy added to it:

"Oh no! he is the village hen. After climbing up the tree at six it's impossible for him to come down before six, the next morning."

He couldn't speak Creole like all others and yet he was always eager more than others to express himself in the language. I couldn't do otherwise than using couple of words in every sentence of his. Taleb was the next to speak:

"You have to be with us at all cost. Because according to our programme we will be grilling the maize at your brinjal field. And after all if you will not be with us we will not be safe. You can reveal our names during enquiries."

I protested:

"Have I ever done things like that?"

After another long discussion everyone came to the conclusion that on Sunday Rooplall would leave his field by midday so one o'clock on Sunday was more appropriate. The suggestion came from Phillipe who said that on Sunday afternoon the fields were deserted. Ultimately I had to be along with.

Two days after came Sunday. The seven of us arrived at Rooplall's field by one thirty, we plucked more than a dozen corns and uprooted almost same quantity of groundnut plants. Soneet had brought along with him a cauldron, salt and a bottle of water. In the sunshine we fixed our hearth under a mango tree. We boiled the peanuts first and then having got embers out of the burnt woods we placed a couple of maize for grilling. We were not at least aware in moments of our rejoicing that the aroma of grilled corn was widely spread. We were still cherising the hot groundnuts and the two last maize were being grilled on the embers when someone appeared at the distance. I didn't take time to recognize Dayanand's father who was returning home after fishing. It was the aroma of grilled maize that brought him to us. All of us stood up and ran away at breakneck speed. In the evening, we all had our different taste of groundnut and corn at home. I got an unforgettable punishment but not as original as that of Soneet. His father had placed the cauldron in front of him and made him eat the whole bulk of some three kilo groundnuts. It was four days later that we came to know of it when he was recovered of his diarrhoea.

Stone Shoes

The girl who, for the first time, took me along to school was known to the school children by the name of Chetwa. This daughter of our neighbour Lamka Dewa's wife, from her first marriage, was five years older than me. My mother, after having entrusted me to Chetwa, had asked her to take good care of me. And if, by chance, since then girls happened to be around me showing keen interest it was perhaps due to that very request. But then it has also proved a prime factor to both my failures and successes.

The shop of Deoduth Gobin, from where we used to have our foodstuff, was more than half mile away from our house. The place was and is still known as *"Teen Bootikya"*, that is Trois Boutiques, but with only two shops. There might have existed three shops sometime back. My father had, a day before, talked to the shopkeeper and it was from him that Chetwa had acquired for me my first slate, a very short-lived one. The school where I had to be admitted was Maheshwurnath Aided School, nearly a mile afar. At that time the school was of two buildings. The first one was of stone walls with roof of corrugated iron sheets and the second, the oldest one, very like a long hangar was thatched with dry sugar cane leaves. My father had contacted Chattar master, the head-teacher, prior to my admission but when Chetwa had taken me to him I was scared of his baldness and his headteacher's seriousness on his face. My fear vanished only when after patting my back he did mention my father's name:

'So you are the son of Pateesingh. All right, you have to be a good child. Try to study like your brother Jaddoo."

I had never known my eldest brother. He was born of my father's first marriage and my mother was the second wife of my father after the death of the first wife. My brother Jaddoo was the first Government teacher in the locality. Whoever had known him still talks of his intellectual abilities, a quality that went uninherited by me. I was the slowest coach in schools. A framed photo of my brother, taken a few months before his sudden death, by a famous photographer of the time, Rakshasingh, was hanging on the raffia wall of our house. It happened one day that the frame was dropped down and its glass dashed to pieces. I was slapped for it by my father. I do not think that the frame got dropped by itself. My parents used to praise my late brother in such a way that I had a feeling of having something pinching in me. May be it was jealousy. And there is no doubt that in order to come out of the inferiority complex I might have easily said to my parents:

"You will see I will surpass his fame."

Poverty had started in our house before the starting of my school days. I was given one cent by my mother as pocket money. The day when bread was not available my mother would compensate me with one more cent, value for half bread and a light spread of cheap margarine. The pocket money given to me, on several occasions, had either got lost or stolen away. With empty stomach I could do nothing but have my eyes fixed on the meals of others. Persisting hunger made me run to the tap to have my stomach filled with water.

In school, the first song which I was taught along with other pupils was an English song whose meaning I came to know much later. The song that we were asked to go on singing in unison, without understanding, was—"Rule Britannia, Britannia rules the waves .... Britons never shall be slaves." As though we the slaves were bound to pray for our sovereign state who had at its mercy some fifty-two colonies. It was perhaps because of the constant prayers of the innocent children throughout the colonies that Britain, holding the destinies of us all, was spared from becoming dependent to any one.

I was of a very shy character in my school days and even now I have managed to give up only half of that timidity. My first lady teacher used to tease me by saying—"You girl-looking!" Despite my not liking the remark I had to accept it as a compliment. When back home I went straight to the old mirror but even that bias reflection in it seemed echoing the same remark. It was my youngest sister (among my four sisters) who was scolded after the cracking of the mirror to pieces. And that temper I still have it.

We had to go to school on foot. The long tarred road from

our house to the school became heated in the summer afternoon. It was very difficult for us to walk on it barefooted. There were very few children who had wooden "*sa-vattes*" in their feet and hardly a dozen, amongst the five hundred children, who wore shoes. Our feet got burned by the heated road and blisters came out on our soles. Walking became hard.

One of our friends had got an idea and as from the next day we all found an easy way to protect our feet from the heat of the tarred road. There was a "Lassora tree" (Pied Lacole) with bunches of longan-like fruits producing a thick paste. After the "genial" idea of one of our friends, we had already started having in our possession dried stones of mango (Loyo mangue). One of us had to climb the 'pied lacole' and come down with bunches of the paste-providing fruit. After having spread the fruit's paste on the dry mango stones we had them stuck on our soles. Thus having two mango stones, rear and front, on each sole of our foot we walked safe enough on the heated tarred road. Our steps were then as arrogant as those wearing real shoes. We had to do it only in the afternoon because in the morning the road was of normal temperature.

By walking on the heated road with our stone shoes we were, of course, spared of burns but because of the shoes we were compelled to reduce our walking speed. We were reprimanded at home for returning late. But the reprimand was not as painful as walking barefoot on the burning road. It was not only the burnings of our feet that were soothed but also the pair of our hearts.

Our little hearts did get the solace of the fact that it was not only for the children of the rich walk with the horse hoof noise but for us too, though in our own way.

Slices from a Life

Hospitality Vended

Luchmee was my cousin who was brought up in our house like several other children. I, too, called her Luchmee because I heard everyone around calling her by that name. This was not liked by my parents yet I never called her "*Didi*". She was the youngest of my two elder sisters and two to three years older than my third sister. Things which I did not know at that time were that she used to take me from my mother's bed to lull me to sleep along with her. I was then being fed on my mother's milk. When deprived of the warmth of my mother's embrace, I started crying. Luchmee wrapped herself along with me in my mother's saree and sang to me the lullaby my mother used to sing when I refused to sleep. I was also told that it was again Luchmee who taught me to walk my first steps by making me hold her finger. But things which I knew by myself and still remember are those of three or four years later. Pinching my cheeks was one of her habits.

Luchmee entertained me to meal by giving me the first morsel from her *thali* before starting herself. I had to continue sleeping on her bed until the day she got married and left our house. I was then seven years old. The separation was very painful to me and it became more painful when I heard my parents talking about how she was ill-treated and battered by my brother-in-law whom I started scaring. My parents had no alternative but to have Luchmee back amongst us.

Two years later she was remarried. This time my brother-in-law was lame but he hadn't a dreadful face like the former one. Despite his good-looking he hadn't half the charm of Lutchmee. He had two twin daughters from his earlier marriage who were of my age. Both embarrassed me undeliberately by addressing me "*Mamoo*", that is uncle. It had to be like this even later on when J.N. Roy, Teeluck Callychurn and Bikramsingh Ramlalah, with almost my double age called me "*Mamoo*" because my father was their "*nana*", grandfather.

After the marriage of all my four sisters, including Luchmee who was to me more sister than my three sisters, my parents had to live in dire straits. Our little tobacco shop was closed for months because my father could not say *'For credit come tomorrow'* — to his customers. Worries multiplied for my parents because my younger sister met with the same fate that of Luchmee. The family in which she was married was good and well-off one but the mother-in-law was very cruel to my sister. She was my father's most loving child. He could not leave her to suffer, so like Luchmee she too was brought back. A younger brother of mine, Dushyant, had died and the last one, Dhruv, was born whom everybody called the "*Petponchooa*", meaning the last of the womb. I was the tenth amongst the eleven children of my mother. Days started becoming so hard that my mother had to raise two cows and compelled to go twice per day for their fodder. Despite the overwork of my mother, life was not easy for us. It became worse when one of our cows became sterile. My mother's burden could have been less by selling the cow but she refused to sell it to the butcher. Even amidst our scarcity-stricken days we were happy to know that Luchmee was well-treated in her second home in Rose-Hill. Her father-in-law, always in urban attire, was an Arya Samaji strict on certain matters but very kind to her. Lutchmee had to address him as "*Peetajee*" instead of the common address Papa and I was also asked to address him in the same way. My brother-in-law was electrician in a sugar factory owing to which the family had an affluent enough life. The whole family had the habit of visiting us almost every two months coming by taxis.

When they had just started coming days were not much bad for us. My mother had all the time, kept aside in a basket, a few eggs laid by a few hens bred by her. These eggs were left to accumulate and were sold in moments of great need. It helped my mother to solve certain urgent and instant problems. But then there happened to be situations with neither any eggs nor any forgotten cent to be seen in the whole house when suddenly the Rose-Hill family was at the door. And it was my mother who was the most worried of all of us.

Knowing our situation *Peetajee* continued visiting us with the same zeal. After having formally met everyone in the family he would go straight to the kitchen and, without letting

Slices from a Life

any member of his family know, put two or three ten-rupee notes on the old wooden table. A sum sufficient to provide, at that time, food for at least two dozens people. To the hesitation of my mother he would say:

"You are now my sister and how could I go from my sister's house without having a good lunch?"

Without waiting for any explanation from my mother, *Peetajee* would go to my father to continue their unending discussion on either religion or history. I was to stand by my mother and see her hand trembling and eyes full of tears but without any of them dropping down. A few minutes had to pass before she handed me the money and ordered the list. Hardly half an hour of my return from the Chinese shop and the vegetables vendor, the air would be filled with aroma coming out of our kitchen. An aroma different to our usual cooking.

And when after a stay of four to five hours our guest had gone, my mother let the retained drops fall from her eyes. My little sister was the only one to console her. My father and my younger brother had never seen those tears coming out my mother's eyes. I was, every time, pained by it but at the same time I silently wished Luchmee and her family to come more regularly so that I could get the special cuisine of my mother more often.

The Big Save

It was the time when the "Indian National", football team of Triolet, was very famous in the north. Much after the good days of "Sangram" and prior to "Hindu Rovers". The former's playground was at 7eme Mile and the latter's behind Maheshwarnath Aided School. I had attended a few matches of the "Sangram" team one of which was against the British navy team, the Glasgow. But I wasn't so must a devoted fan of "Sangram" as I was of the "Indian National" whose goal-keeper was Ah-Sin, a shopkeeper in Ah-Piang's shop. He was very agile and the other three players of the team who I was very fond of were Deven, Gyan and Gopi. The playground of the team was nearly three miles away from my house and despite the long walking distance I made it a must to be present on all important matches along with my friends. I very earnestly wanted to be a very good goal-saver as Ah-Sin and a very good goal-scorer like Deven.

At the extreme part of Triolet where I lived there was a literary youth association by the name of Triolet North Youth Club. I was one of the members who proposed to have sport section in the club and our first sport activity was football. We used to play in an instant playground of Bhogun's estate, a place where there used to be the first cinema hall of the village. It was by mere coincidence that the second cinema hall was to be situated near the playground of my favourite team, the 'Indian National'. I was then of twelve or thirteen and as dull in sport as in learning. In those days there was in the neighbourhood Government School of Trou-aux-Biches a teacher whom we knew as Monsieur Ruhee. One day he arranged for a match between the pupils of his school and members of our club. We posted a few handwritten posters announcing the great match owing to which we got a good crowd. As I was not too good a player I was selected on rare occasions to play in serious matches. It was only when the team was not complete of the bests. Their bad luck was my good luck and I was posted as centre forward in the place of

Slices from a Life

Taleb who was on visit to his grandmother. I was a better goalkeeper but the empty place of Taleb was that of the scorer so I gladly accepted Jowaharlal's offer who was the captain.

Before the starting of the game, I started imagining myself in the place of Deven, the scorer of Indian National. I thought of his style of dribbling and reaching the goalpost with similar speed to score. During the first quarter hour of the match I was given three good opportunities to score. The first ball I got from Vidyanan which instead of shooting straight to the goalpost I wanted to dribble in order to reach to a more reliable position. I succeeded in passing two opponents but then I was suddenly stopped by the able bodied stopper. Jowaharlal was furious on my missing the hit. The second chance was provided by Jowaharlal himself. He jumped higher than the tall player of Trou-aux-Biches team and with a well-controlled head, sent the ball straight to my right foot. I ran forward with the ball between my feet, went closer to the keeper and yet failed to throw the ball in between the two aloe poles. I just stopped seeing the ball going much upward and Jowaharlal was once again full of reprimand.

After being twice scolded, I got blushed and yet didn't give up the urge of scoring. The third ball was again passed to me by Vidyanan. This time I attempted a very precise shot in the exact direction. It was no doubt a very well calculated and sharp one but the tall goalkeeper appeared from the extreme right catching the swinging ball in his lap. It was indeed a very fast move on his part to stop my shot from reaching its target. The public applause which was destined to be mine went roaring for him. Our team had superior number of spectators and many of them started hooting at me.

The visiting team had an advantage of two goals on us. A few players in our team were as though disheartened. In the half time period Jowahar was surrounded by all the players of Triolet North Youth. He advised us not to be discouraged and gave us some new hints and tactics. On the request of Vidyanan, who was the elder of all of us, the captain ordered me to change my post and take that of the goalkeeper. In our days it was often like this. I had no alternative than to accept the decision. Before the starting of the second time I was in the mid of the two poles. After having a brief discussion with the players of the front lines the captain came to me and said:

"You missed three times and made us lose three goals. We, the forwards, will try our best to return the two goals to the boys of Monsieur Ruhee. It is up to you to prevent them from scoring any more.

He repeated the same advice to Philip and Prem who were the two stoppers in my left and right. I talked to myself and tried to gather certain confidence to the fact that Hareea, the previous goalkeeper, had already taken the blow of two goals but I have to see to it that I do not allow any more goal. I have to prove to our fans that if I happened to miss three goals, I can at least make myself accepted as a good keeper by good savings.

It was only after the start of the second time that I became aware of the sun just in front of me with glazing rays on my eyes. It was an obstacle that blurred the visuality but not a reason to take away my determination from me. In the first fifteen minutes of the second time I got an avalanche of direct and indirect shots but I came out as a good saver. And next as it was calculated by our captain Hasen from our side succeeded in scoring the first goal for our team. There was a roaring applause from our fans. Our team was now confident to obtain a draw and attempt a victory.

The following half hour was a real tug of war between the two teams but despite all attacks there wasn't any goal from either side. Because of the two defenders in front of me I didn't get any dangerous shot but still I happened to stop a few tremendous shots for which I got long clapping and cheers from the spectators. We were playing the remaining fifteen minutes of the match when Vidyanan failed to control his position on an aerial shot. The ball was ultimately stopped by an opponent with the chest and immediately sent to his fellow in front of him. Hareea who was around tried to interfere but the one with the ball was faster. I watched him approaching me after leaving all my friends behind. He was at about fifteen feet from the goal when he slowed down to have a well aimed shot. Vidyanan who was a good runner came by him and tried to have possession of the ball. During the interference the ball went upward and was touched by Vidyanand's hand. The referee whistled and declared a penalty. In spite of all the protest of our team the ball was brought to the penalty line. Though the sun had come down, its rays were still straight in my eyes. Before the penalty kick took place Jowahar came by my side and whispered in my ears:

"You rather concentrate to your right. His shot is sure to be to the right."

I stood in the mid of the poles with all readiness to throw myself to the right for the save. The rays of the sun were dazzling before my eyes. The whistle went on. The player chosen for the penalty kick was ready for it and he reached the ball in a very cool way and shot. But then what happened were the least expected. The ball swung forward and along with it the shoe of the kicker also took the same direction. In those days very few players used to wear football shoes. It was the days of *Passtalon* prior to the *Tiptop* and almost every player was in the habit of wearing ordinary tennis shoes which we called *Passtalon*. With the swinging of the ball and the *Passtalon* I, as advised by my captain, threw myself to the right. . . And at the very next second I had in my hands the *Passtalon* of the penalty kicker. The ball with a faster speed than the shoe went straight through the left corner into the goal and from there to the cane field at the back.

My First Pair of Shoes

I cannot forget my first visit to Port Louis for, at least, three reasons. The first one is because of the amazement I had in seeing for the first time a world different to what I had been seeing everyday for nine years. The second, being the most memorable of the three, was because I got on that occasion my first pair of shoes. My mother, after having sold one of the goats from our enclosure, had given thirty rupees out of the forty to my father to purchase clothes for my sisters and shoes for me. Before coming to the third reason that makes my first day in the town an unforgettable event, let me come to the visit itself.

The bus by which my father and I travelled from Triolet to Port-Louis was either Commander III or Commander IV. At that time the arrival terminal for the northern buses was near the Jummah Mosque in Royal Road. At the very entrance itself I was enthralled by the buildings and the hustle-bustle of the streets. Everything was so different compared to what I was seeing everyday. I had heard much about "Shahar", the town, from my parents and was all the time so willing to see everything with my own eyes. When my father, holding my hand, made me cross the first street I was still looking at the white mosque with amazement.

After going through a straight narrow lane we reached another street as large as the Royal Road. My father told me that it was the Desforges Street from where we were supposed to buy clothes for my sisters. The shops were mostly general retailers and solely of cloth. We had to move from shop to shop till my father was able to find out the cheapest market price he was looking for. I found his bargaining very boring. He would advise me from time to time not to fix my eyes on the shop windows and buildings while walking and to be careful of the unevenness of the footpath. I showered questions to my father throughout in order to get the maximal explanation from him of all the things around. When we reached near the attractive place, told to me by my father to be the Municipality Hall, I started another series of questions such as to whom belongs such a beautiful place, what is meant by Mayor! It was then that a group of youngsters laughed at us, made fun of my father's *dhoti* and the language in which we, father and son, were conversing. My father advised me to stop talking in Bhojpuri, the village language, and I was really surprised by both the abhorrence shown by those youngsters and the polite order of my father. My mood was suddenly changed and it took us about two hours to buy the required clothes. My pair of shoes was still to be bought and my impatience was rising to crescendo.

My bare feet had started giving me an inkling of irritation. I saw for the third time a "*carriole*" which was much more attractive that the village oxcarts. I once again expressed my desire to travel by the "*carriole*" which this time was accepted by my father. We were still in Desforges Street when, with my good luck, my father succeeded in stopping an unoccupied one being pulled by a white horse. I was lifted to the seat by my father. What a pleasant trip it was though not long enough. We went to the gigantesque Champ-de-Mars and from there we were taken back to Corderie Street for a fare of thirty cents.

I was hungry but I wanted my shoes first. My father did it the other way and took me to a Gujarati sweetshop in Corderie Street. It was a very neat place with a framed picture of the Goddess Lakshmi on the wall. Smell of hot *Bhajeea* being fried in pure ghee made me forget the burning desire for shoes at least for a few minutes. One of the two tables was wholly occupied so we had to move to the rear one and sit on the long bench occupied by only one person. My father ordered for half pound of "*Garam Bhajeea*" and half pound of "*Samoossa*". It was the cookies shop my father used to talk very praisingly. We finished our light lunch with tea as tasty as the *Bhajeea* and *Samoossa*.

Compared to the vastness of my everyday surroundings some of the streets were narrow and dense. It made me wonder about how the rays of the sun could enter the houses and the buildings. Which really pleased me were riot of colours and movements. The streets were hot yet so alive. I saw to my amazement an old Chinese woman carrying two full tins of I don't know what on her shoulder with the help of a long bamboo. We also visited the Central Market where everything was vibrant and live amidst the noise and the chaos. My father augmented the eagerness in me for my shoes by talking for some half an hour with an acquainted vegetables seller.

And at last, to my great satisfaction, we entered a Chinese shop situated in a narrow street. It was the great moment. My father purchased my first pair of shoes after I tried the size. The colour was brown and shining. At home I had on several occasions attempted at wearing the two big shoes of my father but the real sensation was when I made my first step out of the shop with leather smell. I walked in the street with unusual heavy steps and yet as proud as a peacock. After hardly walking for some fifteen minutes I started feeling that my feet were being pinched but I said nothing to my father.

My father took me to the statue of Labourdonnais and from there to the waterfront where a huge crane was unloading a ship. There were two men on top of it conducting the manoeuvre. I saw for the first time a train passing. I was so near that it terrified me. The pinching of the shoes was increasing. My father seemed to know the fact but when he wanted the confirmation I said that it was alright.

After having shown me the harbour and the main part of Port-Louis that give a vivid picture of the commercial activity of the country my father ultimately thought of returning home. The northern bus station was in Jummah Mosque Street. When we reached there, a bus had just left. We were told that the next bus was scheduled to leave for Triolet only after getting full and that may take a whole hour. The pain in my feet was becoming unbearable. There were two tea-shops shown as "*l'hotel du the*" near the bus stand. Both seemed to be in competition with each other not only in influencing the waiting passengers but also in the offering of their musical numbers. Their gramophones, playing from one side a song of K.L. Saigal and from the other side a song of Johra, were volumed to such a loud pitch that it was difficult to distinguish the lines. My father took me inside one of the teashops that was playing the Saigal's song, his preference not mine.

When the bus came we entered and remained sitting for another half an hour before leaving Port Louis so deeply engraved in my mind. And now the third reason that has kept my first day in the town ever alive, it was because what happened the next day when I went to school. The teacher was writing a few arithmetic problems on the board. A subject in which I was the most dull in the class. When the teacher turned to the class he caught me giving a detailed "*reportage*" to my classmates of all the new things I had seen in Port Louis. I was already reprimanded and punished for my absence of the day before. Those were the days of *Rotin Bazar* and the way I was inflicted the punishment on that day was the worst I have ever known. It was a non-stop slashing for at least a whole minute and being not enough I was put to stand on the bench with my hands up for the whole period of Arithmetic. So this is the third reason to make my first day in Port Louis an unforgettable event.

Days of Toys

Throughout my childhood and my youth I did my best to keep myself happy despite all the sadness around me. It was a period when happiness was just like footnotes on the pages of my life so how could I let those limited and precious moments to be swallowed by dejection and melancholy which was so abundant. In a very natural way I did let myself go happy and lucky with whatever available and in whatsoever situation. The greatest wish of a child has been, all the time, of having as many toys as possible, things which I did not get and yet was not sad for.

The very first toy of my childhood days was a wooden horse cart. I cannot say of children living in towns but for those living in villages, this wooden cart, with a little tin horse, used to be a very precious belonging. Whenever the elders of the houses were to go to the Champ-de-Mars for the races, with their dark umbrellas in hands, the children would go on repeating their requests to bring for them the so cherished 'Calèché', that is the wooden horse cart. Very few children had this wish of theirs fulfilled and those who had them were the most privileged of the village and also the most proud. I was among those children who got their cart after constant requests for months. It was a cold afternoon when my father on his return from the races had in his hands the little wooden cart in variegated colours. Its long wooden handle for pushing purpose was of red colour. When pushed forward the horse and the rider with his jockey's cap would go up and down with the sound of a ringing bell. I was so happy with the toy that I ran to all the houses in the vicinity to show my friends my pride possession and before the sunset I was able to do so. It would have been difficult for me to sleep at night were I not been able to do it.

My father did not have any particular liking for the races. His going to the Champ-de-Mars was always linked with some particular work in the town. For his return home he would see to it that he had with him the usual cookies such as

'*Bhajia*'. *Neemki*' and '*Jelebi*'. The day he brought me my horse cart he also had with him the cookies wrapped in an old newspaper with cotton thread all around. I was always the first to have my share of the cookies but with the toy in my hand did not show any interest for even a single *Bhajia*. The toy was my treasure but unfortunately it did not last for more than one week. It started by the collapsing of the jockey and then two days later it was the turn of the horse to fall down and before the end of the week the wheel gave up as well. But in spite of its short life the horse cart gave me great delight and for one week I was as proud as a prince.

The second toy of my childhood days, for which my friends envied me so much, was my kite. It was a bit strange that we the village children called a kite a '*Telengi*' when it was known as '*Patang*' in creole—'*Patang*' being a Hindi word. It was my brother-in-law from Port Louis who made the real good kite for me which was of red and white colours. He was the chauffeur of barrister Veerasamy Ringadoo. Whenever, after dropping his employer to certain places, my brother-in-law happened to come to our place in the light green car, the neighbouring children got gathered around it in amazement. Coloured cars were rare in those days. I do not remember the make of the car, it might have been an 'Austin Cambridge' but the plate number I still remember was 1326.

It was a time when kite flying was very popular. My friends used to fly their kites in the open place of the eastern part of our houses. It was a place between two rows of sugar cane fields with narrow path for the oxcarts. In between the deep marks left by the carts' wheels there were spots of green grass on which the children stood to cope with each other in sending their kites higher and higher. Emulating my friends I did try on different occasions to make my own kite but none of them was able to stay in the air. When my brother-in-law came to know of it he promised me one and on his second visit to us he brought me the wonderful kite which was a matter of pride to me. My friends' kites were unable to cope with it. Mine was more beautiful and a high-flyer. It made me forget my hunger. But like my wooden cart my kite also did not last for long. The day it cut its string and went with the wind in the direction of the sea I, with a couple of friends, ran after it but in vain. I cried the loss.

My third toy was a wooden top.

Dhanrajwa of our village, who because of his height was known to us as 'Chingree', was an expert in crafting tops. He would select the most appropriate piece of wood from a guava branch, in order to make his skilful tops. He painted them in different colours and gave them names of his liking. His favourite top that spinned for long like a whirlwind was called '*Lalleea*' because of its red colour. In the same way his second favourite green top was called '*Hareea*'. He agreed to craft a beautiful one for me with the condition that I let him pick mangoes from the mango tree in front of our house. He painted my top (with a gramophone needle in its bottom) in blue stripes and called it '*Neeleea*'. Traffic at that time was very less and sometimes it would take a full half-hour before a vehicle would pass. Chingree, Premwa, Ismael, Philippe and Dadibal were among my elder friends with whom I participated in the top spinning race.

The whip used by us to spin the top was made of aloe fibre. There was an aloe fibre factory in the way to the seaside not very far from our houses. Chingree himself brought those fibres for all of us and he himself braided the whips and tied them to filao's rods. Our method of making our tops spin very effectively was by winding the whip around the upper part of the top. After that holding the winded top along with the rod—we laid it on the tarred road. Then we threw it to a certain distance and the top started spinning. In order to keep it going on we had to slash it with the whip. This slashing made the toy jump to a longer distance and spin faster. Nobody was ever able to cope with Chingree in maintaining the spinning longer and faster. Our race started from 'Kalimaye' to reach 'Neuviememille' but in that long course it was only Chingree's top that was capable of a return journey. Ours had to fall down and restart for more than once.

My top '*Neeleea*' was one of the best that Chingree had been able to produce. With the whip in the wizard hand of Chingree my '*Neeleea*' also had once completed a non-falling return journey from 'Kalimaye-Neuviememille-Kalimaye'. Like my other toys this top too had to go away from me. One day it was stolen. But my attachment to it was so deep that even the change of colour, by one of my friends who stole it, did not stop me from recognizing it on the road, though weeks later. Even up to now that friend of mine is not aware of the fact that my '*Neeleea*' was in his possession. Hope he will not go through this copy of *Le Mauricien*.

The Outcast That I Am

I know that this slice will provoke the wrath of a few people but as it is a bitter truth of my childhood, I am producing it here in all humbleness. It is once again excerpted from my book "*Atma Vigyapan*" published in New Delhi in 1984 in which I haven't allowed any auto-censor. People of my age bear witness to the monster of the past which has today converted itself into a bigger monster known as the class and allegiance discrimination.

The *mantras*, the sacred verses whispered in my ears by my Guru during the rituals of my *Janev*, the sacred thread ceremony, hardly brought to me any knowledge. I was at that time between nine and ten years of age. Neither the *mantras* had any sense to me nor did I understand anything by the taking rounds of the pavilion before proceeding to Kashi to study for a few minutes. The *mantras* of my preceptor Pandit Karnath Chowbe didn't impart any teaching to me, and yet it was at his place that I got the great lesson.

The daughter of my preceptor, who was to be accepted by me as my sister by virtue of preceptoral affinity, was indeed very beautiful. Some three to four months after my initiation the marriage ceremony of my preceptor's daughter Manti Devi was to take place. In those days Hindu marriages were performed mostly at night and it happened to be on any day of the week implementing with the *Lagan*, that is the auspicious wedding moment. Today the auspicicus moment falls only on Sundays to facilitate matters for the officiating priest and there is hardly an auspicious moment at night nowadays. It matters less because I have to tell about that day when I really got the great lesson.

The ceremony of Manti's marriage was that of a grandiose celebration. I had never seen, in my ten years, such great preparations before. There was another huge tent erected by the pavilion known as Marro. The invitees were being requested to the dinner as from five in the evening. We were a group of six or seven friends whose leader was Vijyanand.

We were told that the musical programme was to start after six o'clock, so Vijyanand had suggested that we should sit with the first group for our dinner. Jawahar had already informed us that there were among the curries *karhi barhi*, *kachoo*, and other vegetables. He also told us of tamarind's *Takkar* and mangoes' pickles. It was enough for our mouths to get salivated. We all gathered around Vijyanand to joint the first group being requested to sit on the mats. There were two hosts who were choosing and approaching the guests for the first round. We went straight to the dining tent without being requested by the hosting people. The arrangement was for forty persons each time. There were already some thirty guests sitting with banana leaves in front of them when we seven boys joined them. It was Soneet's father who distributed banana leaves amongst us. I was still trying to sit comfortably on the mat when an obese person came to us. He held me by my shoulder and took me away from the dining place along with my friend Soonooa. He then told us that we shall be sitting for our food when our turn comes. Vijya and Jawahar pleaded with the obese man to let the two of us sit for the dinner but it was of no use. He told them very bluntly that it was the turn of the highest caste.

Soonooa and I remained outside, and I started thinking of the reason how our other five friends were taken for the highest caste and why not we two as well. Then my attention went on the dress of Soonooa and I also looked at mine.

It became clear to me that we were outcast because of our shabby dress. Soonooa and I were not in attire to be able to sit along with the highest caste. We remained outside and watched a second group going for the feast. It was after an hour or so when the third group was invited I pushed my friend forward and we joined the group. We had hardly taken our seats on the mat when the obese person appeared again and took us away by saying that it was the turn of the higher caste. I told him that I was the son of Pattee Singh, the most respected person of the areas.

The obese wasn't interested to any explanation. He took us by our arms and threw us outside. After the higher caste came the turn of the high caste and it was much later that the remaining group with hunger twisting inside was asked to sit for dinner. The obese man welcomed us by saying:

"Come! Take your seat and eat as much as you can."

On that day and at that very instant I came to learn what I missed from my preceptor during my "*Janev ceremony*". And it was at his door itself. I was instantly taught that a man in tattered dress hasn't the right to be of a decent family.

Many years later when I joined the cultural institute, where I am still attached, my superior convened me in his office and reproached me of my not being properly dressed. He said:

"You are looking like an outcast amongst all the head of departments."

I smiled at his remark and said in a subordinate's voice:

"Even the outcast have a place in the realm of Mahatma Gandhi."

Money Bearing Tree

When I first heard my mother using the phrase "money bearing tree" it was during those days when I was still wearing my first long-worn half-pant. On the other side of the main road opposite our house was the most attractive, and well-off looking house of the locality. In its Maison Creole style it had its roofs of corrugated iron-sheets painted in red and with walls of well-chiselled stones. Its veranda was of wood with glass panes. It belonged to Shamlal, the blacksmith, and which was known as "p'tit chateau". It happened that one day 1 asked my mother how was it that our house was walled by ravenals and roof thatched of dried cane leaves while Samlal *bhaiya's* house was so different, so beautiful. My mother who was at that time angry with my sister said to me in the very same tone:

"One should have a money bearing tree to have such a great house."

Having heard of the "money bearing tree" I went on thinking about it the whole night. When I asked my sister to tell me if really such tree exists she pinched both my cheeks and said stressing on each word:

"Yes. But one has to labour very hard for it."

"And what if after hard labour the tree grows and starts bearing coins?"

"Then you have to go on shaking the tree and the ground gets covered with coins."

The next day I asked my friend Soonoo;

"Have you ever seen a tree bearing money?"

"I haven't seen but am told that in the courtyard of the sugar estate owner there are several such trees."

"But how is it that in the courtyard of Premwa, whose father happened to have the most beautiful house in the area, hasn't any?"

"This I don't know."

"Do you know how to grow a money-tree?"

"In the same way like other trees."

Slices from a Life

"But trees grow out of seeds. Does money also have any seed?"

"I think that in order to grow a coin-tree one has to grow the coin itself."

Soonoo's last sentence made sense to me. It was mere coincidence that my aunt of Cottage visited us the day after. While going back in the afternoon she, as usual, gave me two coins of five cents each. Each time he had given me money before leaving our house I had immediately run to Michel's shop to buy *moolkoo* or sucre d'orge but this time I gazed at the coins in my palm with another desire. I was wishing them to grow into two trees and had their branches laden with coins.

Though our house was nothing but a three-room hut my sister always had it embellished by planting flowers around. She used to have a few earthen pots in front of the house in which I grew special plants of her choice. I went near the pots and with the help of a stick I made a two-inch deep hole in each of the two with more apparent space. Having put one coin in each hole I covered them with layers of soil. After two days, evading the sight of my sister, I dug the two flower pots to find out any sprouting. This manoeuvre went on for a whole week and each time I was disappointed by not seeing any sprout at all. The next morning I asked my sister:

"When you put a seed under the soil how many days does it take to sprout out?"

"There are seeds which came out in three or four days and others take ten to fifteen days."

The answer gave me new hope. I had enough grey matters in my head to at least understand that the coin being very hard couldn't sprout so easily like a bean. I always watched my father doing his kitchen garden in the backyard. Once I had asked him the reason of the two tiny flags amidst the plantation and to which he had replied.:

"The white flag is meant to keep birds away and the second is to spare the plants from evil eyes."

Reminded of it I also fixed a small red flag in each of the earthen pots. My sister saw them and asked me the reason:

"Why these red flags?"

And prior to any hesitating reply from me she took them out from the pots and throwing them away scolded me:

"I do not want you to touch my flower pots. You have

made my geraniums wither."

I stood by the two pots with sadness in my eyes when Soonoo coming from behind stood by my side. He watched me looking at the flower pots and then asked me:

"What are you looking at? Are you not joining us to play police and thief game? They have already started it."

"It seems that these coins will never grow."

"What did you say?"

"I planted two *Cinq sous* in these two pots. None of the two seems to grow."

Soonoo stayed silent for a while and then asked:

"It got how many days?"

"More than seven."

"Do you water them every day?"

"My sister does it from time to time."

"But you have to water them everyday, otherwise they will never grow. And after all it is you who have planted them and it is you who should take care of them. If you manage to water them both in the morning and the afternoon the sprouts will come out in matter of days. Go and bring a watering can full of water."

I listened to his advice and ran for the water. I went to the place where my sister Tiffi was cleaning the kitchenwares. In order not to make myself seen by her I went slowly behind her to pick up the watering can. The can was half full with water. I brought it to the pots. Soonoo who was very close to the two pots went a few steps behind to let me water. After having done the job I put down the empty watering can and with a certain self-satisfaction said to Soonoo:

"Let's go now for the game."

"You go, I'll join you in a few minutes."

And he ran in the direction of Michel's shop. Some fifteen minutes later when I was wholly involved in playing the police-and-thief-hide-and-seek with my other friends I saw Soonoo returning home from the shop. He was sucking a green coloured sucre d'orge.

Even the fools are sometimes allowed to jump to conclusion. I brooded for a while and ran to the place where I had to. I looked at the two flowerpots and bending myself by the first one dug out the upper layers of soil and was aback. I dug out half the soil but the five-cent coin wasn't there.

Slices from a Life

I went through the other pot, emptied it completely and the result was the same. Both coins were gone.

I rushed to Soonoo's house but he wasn't available. Soonoo never went to school but I was attending school everyday.

Shares of the Offerings

The three childhood events always stood out in my memory. The triangle was made of my home, the premises of the Maheswarnath Shivala and the seaside at Trou aux Biches. If I was not busy playing "*Gooli Danda*", "*Kabaddi*", football with ball made out of rags or the game of marbles in our yard I was to be found in the temple's vinicity. Swinging from root to root of the widely spread banyan tree we aped Tarzan. I also used to be in the mango orchard behind the temple telling and listening stories among my friends. The third angle of the triangle happened to be the seashore, where swimming in the cool water of the sea and playing on the cotton white sand were great fun for all of us. We also went for fishing amid those rocks not too far from Mont Choisy; which are evergreen in my mind though smashed and bashed to give way to hotels. If there exists real happiness in life it is no doubt that of the childhood days in which there was no difference among Dayanand, Philippe and Taleb. The circle of my friends consisted of some eighteen or twenty boys and whenever we were together it was at least in eight or ten.

The Shivala was then a more accessible place where children were very free to roam and play. Luchmee Pandit was the priest in those days and because of his great affection for children he was definitely different from today's *pujaris*. The members of the committee also never thought of making the temple a fortress. During the religious ceremonies and festivals all hospitality was extended to the public and devotees were served with food and refreshment. The *Khichri* served on those occasions wasn't a treat to be forgotten easily. Collective *puja*, *katha* and *kirtan* were regular features of those religious activities. It was through the encouragement of Luchmee Pandit that I staged my first written play in the Shivala's hall and amidst the mango orchard I wrote my first stories. But the reminiscence being presented here is of an earlier period where I was of eleven or twelve.

My friends and I didn't while away all our time just in

playing or climbing up the mango and longan tree, plucking and eating the ripe fruits but we also used to give a helping hand in sprucing up the premises. Philippe and Taleb always joined us in the same. The event took place during the celebration of the Maha Shivratri. The preparation of the festival would start some fifteen days earlier when Hanif Bhaiya, whom we called Bhaiya Hanif, used to smash coconut on the steps of the main Shiv temple as an offering to Lord Shiva before proceeding to the changing of the yellow banner atop the "*Kalash*" of the temple. Though a Muslim by faith Bhaiya with all daringness and faith was the only person to climb atop and hoist the ceremonial flag. Though we, all the children, were engaged in the cleaning we could not stop ourselves from admiring the great dexterity of Hanif Bhaiya and we gave him long clapping when he came down after accomplishing his big seasonal job.

Maha Shivratri, in spite of its religiosity, was a festival full of fun for all the children around. It came with all usual splendour and ended with the satisfaction of one and all. The next day members of the temple collected all the offerings of the devotees which were in silver coins and a few bank notes from other offerings combined with flowers, "*Pan*" and "*Bel*" leaves. The job of getting rid of the leaves and other remaining *puja* stuff were left to our care. We had to take them from the temples and deposit the whole lot by the old ruin at the rear of the main temple. Despite the great care with which the coins were picked from the leaves and collected by the members of the temple there were always some coins especially those not in silver which were left stuck in between the worshipping ingredients. My pals and I would go through all the petals and leaves to fish out the remaining coins.

We were seven in all on that occasion who after the completion of the cleaning work went straight to the heap. The heap of leaves and flowers was as big as the great number of devotees who came from every part of the island a day before. We started shifting the leaves which still had the smell of camphor and incense very carefully one by one. I hadn't forgotten the search of the last year in which I got ten coins of two cents and three of five. It was enough for my morning show ticket. But the luckiest of us all on that day was Philippe who with the excess of speed in going through the leaves was able to amass a sum of two rupees in all. In those days the daily earning of a labourer was seventy cents to one rupee.

All the seven of us sat around the heap, everyone with a lot for himself in front of him and we started the search by separating leaf from leaf. Premwa was the first to get the first coin which he immediately put in his pocket without showing to anyone. It was Taleb who whispered in my ear to say that it was a twenty five cents silver coin. I had to shift more than twenty *Pan* leaves to come across my first finding a brown coin of two cents. We took more than an hour to move the heap of leaves from one place to another because the leaves and petals were stuck with vermilion and the mixed paste of the offerings consisting of fruits and sweets. We had to go one by one through every petal and leaf in order to get the maximum of coins left as our share. Our hands as well as our pockets had become red with vermillion and offerings. Even our shirts were not spared and that was enough for scolding and punishment at home. But none of us was worried about it.

We all jingling our pockets went to the banyan tree. We sat down on the green grass and started counting our coins. There was one thing that instead of having it in the pocket of my pants I had it hidden under my shirt. Nobody was aware of what it was. When all the counting was over it was known that this time Dayanand was the luckiest to have got the greatest number of coins including two silver coins of fifty cents each and his whole amount was three rupees fifty cents. Soonoo was the big loser while I got a sum of two rupees by adding all the coins. And yet the thing which I hadn't shown to any of my friends was still safe under my shirt. When Dayanand had enough of his jumping and shouting for his win I put my hand slowly under my shirt and what came out in my hand was a note of five rupees smeared with vermilion. Everyone was amazed. It wasn't in the habit of the devotees to put a bank note as offering in front of the idol, but what seemed strange was it's being unseen by the members of the Shivala. Much stranger for me was my luck. I was envied by a couple of friends but then I was instantly cheered by others and it was Taleb who spoke most intelligently:

"Tomorrow the Anand Cinema."

And it was up to Kressoon to inform everyone:

Slices from a Life

"Tomorrow we are having a film of Bhagwan and Baboorao in the matinee show—*Bhoot Bungla.*"

I looked at the seven rupees in my hand. I was very easily capable of providing not only tickets for my friends but also sharing with them peanuts, *samoosas* and lemonade as well. After all the film with Bhagwan and Baboorao as actors was running in our cinema hall for already three weeks and with all my eagerness to see the film I couldn't get a ticket for it from my mother. In the mid of my happiness I didn't think that when I'll reach home I will be scolded by my sister for my dirty shirt and the hand of my sister would automatically go into my pocket. And that is what happened in the afternoon when I reached home—a thing which should not have happened for the sake of my friends. My sister, after fishing out the seven rupees from my pocket, looked at the coins and the fiver with all seriousness and then returned the coins to me. Still holding the five rupee notes in her hand she said to me:

"This is for a new pair of pants and a shirt for you".

The Colour of White

The walls of village houses in those days used to be of dry "raffia", "ravenal" or cane straw covered with dung. Most of these walls were pargeted with white earth from outside. This white earth was obtained from the marshy land by the seaside. It was December and I, after the completion of my six years primary schooling, was enjoying the vacation when the season of digging out of the white earth in the vicinity of Grand Bay and its selling started. On that day my mother wasn't at home. She had gone to visit my aunt who was ill at Cottage, a village in the extreme north. I knew that she would be back home only the day after because the journey was by foot. So I was very free to go wherever I liked and do whatsoever I wanted. My mummy had left the house at six in the morning and it was at seven that the carts of Jagessur *Bhaiya* along with other carts of the village left for Grand Bay. Soonoo was by his father on their own cart and I let myself picked up by Jagessur *Bhaiya*. It was my first chance to go to Grand Bay. In those days the short cut to Grand Bay, known as *Vingt Pieds*, was a rough and rugged one. It was a journey full of jolts in which the cart went on rumbling and rattling with a sound effect of groaning.

I had hardly taken my place on the cart when Jagessur *Bhaiya* wanted to know whether I had taken permission at home or not to which I lied very easily. When we reached the marshy land there were already four or five carts standing by and the cartmen loading the white mud. We had to wait for two cans to have completed their loading in order to take their places from where the loading was not so difficult. After having asked me to hold the bridle of the dark ox with long horns Jagessur *Bhai* lifted his *dhoti* up to his thighs and with the pickaxe in one hand and the bucket in another he went knee-deep into the marsh. He went on digging and filling the bucket with the white mud and handing it to Soonoo's father for quite long before taking his place and having him in his. Now it was his turn to get hold of the bucket from

Soonoo's dad and to have it emptied in the two carts. I started getting fed up with the bad smell of the marshy mud and by remaining stuck by the cart. I had joined them with the idea of roaming and amusing myself but instead of the fun I was getting bored for more than an hour by squeaking "ho! ho!" from time to time in order to prevent the ox from moving to and fro. Having perceived my uneasiness Soonoo's father said to me:

"Don't worry you will get the cost of two buckets."

I knew that the cost of one bucket of the marshy mud was 60 cents and accordingly there was all the possibility of my getting at least one rupee for the job being done by me. Soonoo had already informed me that his father had promised him the same amount. I also knew that our job was not just to look after the ox, it also comprised of calling out the customers as soon as we reach our village—"White earth! Glossy white earth!" We were also supposed to fill the buckets of the customers. When we were on the way to the village Jagessur *Bhaiya* asked me:

"Would you like to have two buckets of white earth or money?"

My answer to the question was very short:

"Money."

Opting for the mud would have been a folly on my part because everybody at home would have easily known how I got it and from whom. After all we still have at our place the white earth we bought last year. When the earth was still muddy my mother would make several balls out of the surplus and leave them to dry. They were to be diluted in water next year to be used for the painting of the walls. There were four balls saved from last year on the wall of our kitchen and there was no need for white mud in our house up to the next year. The balls of white earth we had in our possession were said by my mother to be of best quality because it had in it a slight nuance of blue owing to which the walls were rendered more attractive and glossy. On our way home Jagessur Bhaiya shared his lunch with me. The folded "*faraha*" was stuffed with brinjal and potato curry. Jagessur Bhaiya was on foot holding the bridle and I was on the cart. Soonoo with his father was in front of us. They had started eating their bread earlier. The road we were returning by was red and vermilion with flamboyants' blossom.

The sun was above our head when we entered Triolet. Soonoo and I started calling out the villagers as soon as we reached the first house:

"White earth! Glossing white earth!!"

We stopped at the third house. There were a few women coming to us through the Shivala road with buckets in their hands. I was able to recognise Chando *Bhowji* among them who looked at me with amazement and asked me:

"Since when you have become a cartman?"

I was scared of being reported but when she smiled as usual I was relieved of the sudden fear. Our very first halt happened to be a very good start for we sold seven buckets of the white mud. After crossing the Kalimaye I started to be very cautious because I was to pass through our house and I didn't want my father or my sister to see me on the cart. I started calling out buyers only when our house was left behind. When we reached Neuvieme Mille, our cart was almost half emptied. We hadn't reached the Maheshwurnath Aided School when Soonoo's father sold his last bucket of the white earth and yet his cart remained along with us up to the Anand Cinema. In the meantime I have got my share of one rupee.

On our return instead of going home I went to Sonit's place where I washed my hands and feet and got rid of the white mud over my body before appearing in front of my sister. I had a whole rupee in my pocket which I gropped from time to time to remind myself of my valuable possession. There was a great warmth in that coin of my labour. A dream of a long time now going to be realized. I used to draw pictures in hiding because my mother wouldn't allow me. My sister was very fond of my drawings and asked me to have them coloured but my mother was all the time against my inclination towards drawing. Whenever I asked my mother to purchase a box of colours for me like that of Mohan she scolded me by saying:

"You are sent to school to read and write not to draw."

I went to Michel's shop with my precious rupee and bought the so envied box of seven colours at sixty cents. With the remaining forty cents I went to Hamja's shop and purchased the drawing book I have been seeing for weeks at thirty five cents. I came back home with only five cents in my pocket; still I was happy. Without caring about my hunger

Slices from a Life

I took out my old drawing book and started colouring one of the pictures I have sketched earlier. First it was the colour of the sea, then the colour of the boat.., and then the colour of the sky... and the coconut tree... and went on painting... With colours obtained out of the white colour! I was successful in giving my drawings their deserving colours.

The Nasty Trick

I had to, willingly or unwillingly, involve myself in so many nasty tricks of my friends. But there were instances when, very bluntly, I had to go against them. Ramdeo was neither my friend's friend nor mine for the simple reason that he was our elder. He used to come regularly to our place and was in the habit of doing several jobs for us as from climbing the coconut tree upto bringing dry wood fuel for us. Everyone, in the locality, considered him to be the most gentle boy of the area. He lived in the Shivala Road, not too far from us. His mother also did help us in our domestic works. Ramdeo was her only son. Their house was surrounded by several fruit trees which were full of fruits in their respective seasons that made a few people say in astonishment:

"Look how plenty these are. It is very strange that in houses where there are lot of children to eat, trees do not fructify like this."

My friends would call Ramdeva's mother the miser. Because the mangoes, litchis, longans, guavas and other fruits of her trees got ripe and rotten or they were pecked by birds on the trees but never allowed to be picked by the boys. Those who managed to steal them were so badly cursed by her that their mothers were terribly alarmed and advised their children in the following terms:

"The curse of Ramdeva's mother doesn't go in vain. See to it that you do not steal from her trees."

Whenever I asked my mother of the possibility of a curse to happen true she all the time smiled at the question. Once she asked me another question instead of the smile:

"Have you gone stealing once again from Ramdeva's trees?"

I tried my best to stay away from the conspiracies of my friends to steal from Ramdeva's trees. I even refused to take the stolen longans or the sweet carambolas from my friends. Soneetwa would make fun of me by saying that I was scared of Ramdeva's mother's curse. May be that was the reason I can't say. I have heard my mother saying on several occasions that good people die earlier. When I asked her the reason for it she said that God loves good people and for that reason He wants them by His side a bit earlier. Everybody considered Ramdeva as a good boy and perhaps because of it he suddenly died after an illness of 3 days. He had hardly completed his sixteen years. Several persons talked in several ways on that sudden death of his. A few of them went up to saying that Ramdeva had urinated under a black plum tree (*Jamblon*) at midday and he was the victim of the shrew living inside the tree. Everyone with own version. Jawahur's mother was saying to everyone that some witch had played a trick on him. Whatsoever the truth Ramdeva's death was a blow to us and for days our house remained plunged in sadness. For my mother it was as though she had lost one of her own sons.

My friend, in the leadership of Soonooa, worked out a plot to steal litchis from Ramdeva's fruit grove when it wasn't yet seven days of his death. Kissoonwa was Ramdeva's nearest neighbour. The idea came from Kissoonwa himself who said to us that juice is oozing from the ripe fruits.

He also told us that Ramdeva's mother was all the time mourning her son inside her house with doors closed. I had a look from Kissoonwa's house at the litchi's tree which was as red as a flamboyant tree with bunches of ripe litchis. When all my friends agreed to the proposal of Kissoonwa and Soonooa I was the only one to disagree and I didn't participate in that pilferage. The next day I was told of the failure of the group because of Issa, the poultrymen who had known of the planning. At night when my friends launched their so-called raid Issa instigated his two dogs on them.

From that very moment Kissoonwa started finding ways and means in order to square accounts with Ramdeva's mother and Issa. What the boys wanted was to play some nasty tricks upon them. I was also involved in making fun of Issa. When he came out of his house on his cycle to collect eggs and buy poultry we the boys would hide behind bushes and mislead him:

"O poultry man. We have eggs to sell."

He would stop and we would run away. People of the

locality came out of their houses to reproach him on his continous hooting.

"We don't have any egg to sell. Why are you disturbing us?"

We ridiculed Issa for several days and enjoyed ourselves at his being scolded by the village folks. It was Taleb who came out with the idea of making fun of Ramdeva's mother. It was an afternoon. A *panwaria* (folk singer on the occasion of the birth of a child) used to visit our village twice a week. He wore a red turban on his head and a fez over it. He always carried a *dholak* (drum) along with him.

Stopping from place to place he asked people, especially the children of houses where a child was recently born. After having got the required information he went straight to that house and started beating his drum, singing and dancing at the same time. In between he would take out a *thali* (copper plate) from his *jholi* to add to the music of joy by its vibration. His *thali* would go on ringing and echoing until someone from the house would not come out to fill his *jholi* (mendicant's bag).

When Talebwa stopped the *panwaria* to show him the house of Ramdeva's mother I tried to stop him from doing so but of no avail because my other friends had joined him in the ugly game. Yet I continued trying to have them change their mind. I even approached the *panwaria* and wanted to tell that there hasn't taken place any birth at the house he was being sent to and that it wasn't fair to sing song of happiness in front of a house where somebody died just a few days back. I was suddenly seized by Prem and Soneet. It was indeed impossible for me to free myself from their strong grips. The folk singer swooped on Ramdeva's house and my friends keeping space followed him. When I wanted to scream and warn the *panwaria* Premwa put his hand on my mouth.

The *panwaria* went straight to the threshold of Ramdev's house and started beating his drum and singing. I had to stay by Kissoonwa's house to watch the folksinger singing and dancing as though in dementia. My friends were enjoying the scene and I was feeling pangs of regret. A few minutes later we saw Ramdeva's mother coming out of his house with her hands joined in prayer. She stood by the *panwaria* with tears coming out of her eyes. People in the neighbourhood, hearing the sounds of the *dholak* and *thali*, came out of their houses.

When my friends saw people coming they ran away one by one leaving me alone. Ramdeva's mother was crying and begging the folksinger to stop his song and dance but he was too involved in them to pay heed to the imploration. A few people went to *panwaria* and after reprimanding him were able to stop him. It didn't take much time for everyone to know that it was the deed of the boys.

The next morning my mother took me to Ramdewa's mother where I begged her to excuse me. In the afternoon Talebwa, Premwa, Soneetwa and all others had to go with my mother for their shares of pardon and I saw drops still coming out of the eyes of Ramdeva's mother.

The Game

Amongst my friends Prem was the only one who always had his pocket jingling with coins. He was also the most miser of them all. There were of course two reasons of his having money all the time. Instead of going to school like other children of our locality he worked in the workshop of his father who was an ironsmith. Prem was also the luckiest player of marble game which we played in our premises. We were very cautious of not being seen betting by our parents. We had to play two games in order to win the one cent bet.

There were three places where we used to spend our time during the school vacations. The first was our own yard where if we were not involved in the marble game we were sure to be playing football with a grapefruit as our ball. Sometimes we happened to play "*Gooli Danda*", "*Kabaddi*" or 'hide-and-seek'. The second sport where we spent the full days was the seaside. We didn't have any notion of the time while engaged in swimming or fishing. We were most of the time taken to task for staying away from our houses for such a long time but then the punishment was forgotten overnight. Our third place where we played by swinging on the network of the banyan roots at the Mahashwurnath Temple or imitating our cherished film heroes like Premnath, Ranjan, Errol Flynn and Douglas Fairbanks Jr, all aces of "Cap d'epée".

On that particular day we were some twelve boys playing in the atrium of the Shivala where we were very free at picking "longans" and "mangoes" from the adjacent orchard. In those days Pandit Luchmee was the priest in charge of the temple and the freedom and joy of his time were known to us again. Everyday he would distribute amongst us kernels, bananas and *Mohanbhog*, the offerings. One of the very important events of his days was the "*Satyanarain Katha*" taking place at night on every full moon. On those occasions we stayed around helping him to prepare the "*Prasad*". The "*Katha*" was always attended housefull.

We were very fond of the *pujari* and that was the reason for refusing to believe one of his predictions. A prediction that came true as predicted by Pandit Luchmeeji and we were much grieved. Some of us even cried when it happened. He used to tell us of how one day he would be dying a sudden death, without any prior illness. One day he went up saying that he had come very close to his death and it happened that he died just as he predicted—that is one week later and without any illness.

He was still among us when we were playing in the temple's atrium. My friends and I were imitating a scene from a film in which Ranjan, the fencing master, had a long fight with the king's men. My friend Jawahar was playing the role of Ranjan; I was his supporter and others were the king's men. All of us had wooden swords and we stopped that fight after getting really tired. It was the mango season but the ripening of the fruit hadn't yet started so we picked some unripe ones for our salad. Later on Panditji gave us two ripe mangoes and said:

"These are mangoes ripened before time. I got four from a tree at the back. After offering them to God I am sharing them with you to be shared amongst yourselves."

After slicing the two mangoes with a knife which he had brought with him he gave everyone a slice.

In the evening when we decided to leave the premises Jawahar proposed a picnic party as the next day's programme. It was accepted by everybody because it has been long since we had our last one. As usual we had to contribute for it, according to which Jawahar suggested fifty cents contribution per person. For those who were unable to contribute their shares another contribution was to be done amongst those capable. Jawahar, knowing that I was unable to give my share of the contribution, looked at me. Then Vidyanand, the tallest boy of our group, tried to find out all those who were capable of contributing. Only five persons replied in the affirmative. Jawahar volunteered to give fifty cents on my behalf but there were still six of us who were unable to pay. It was Mohun who wanted to know what should be done to meet the cost.

In the meantime after preparing a list and cost of the provisions for our picnic Jawahar told us that we have to buy at least 25 breads, one can of cheese, some 15 bottles of lemonade, and 4 cans of sardines. The whole cost was of seven rupees. We hadn't to worry for the tomatoes, chillies, onions and salt because these things were supposed to come from our houses. We still had to find out ways and means to get the missing three rupees. Suddenly an idea struck Jawahar and taking me a few steps away he said:

"I think we can get this lacking sum from someone."

"From whom?" I asked him.

"From Premwa."

Mohan who had followed us started laughing.

"From that miser who will be giving his own share of contribution by putting off through pretexts!"

"You just see. I am going to have the three rupees out of his pocket without force."

"How?"

"Don't ask question. Await the event taking place."

We returned in the midst of our friends. The guarantee given to us by Jawahar wasn't as convincing.

After asking for the attention of everybody he said:

"We are short of three rupees for our picnic!"

One of the boys said:

"Premwa was saying that he has in his pocket five rupees. Why not ask him three rupees? We shall return it later on."

To which Prem instantly objected:

"I cannot give because I have to buy a shirt with my money."

"You are lying because you do not want ..."

Jawahar interrupted:

"Look here, let us play a game. He who loses will have to pay the three rupees."

Several boys asked in unison:

"What game?"

Without saying anything further Jawahar took us near the temple. After asking us to stay down the steps leading to the central door of the Shivala he showed the two statues of the tigers on both sides atop the stairs. Then he said:

"Two of us have to put their hands in the mouths of these two tigers. Who can do it?"

The boys said in chorus:

"I can! I can!"

"But listen to me well. We need only two persons for the game—one will have to put his hand in the mouth of the

Slices from a Life 155

tiger on the right and the other person in the mouth of the other one. But there is one condition. He who will insert his hand inside has to take it out smilingly. He who fails to smile will be the loser. Now tell me who among you wants to participate along with me?"

Some four or five boys along with Prem raised their hands. Jawahar continued explaining:

"I repeat it again. He who will take his hand out of the tiger's mouth without a smile will lose and will have to pay three rupees."

Accepting the challenge Prem said,
"Where is the problem in it?"
"Ok, then let the game start between you and me", said Jawahar.
"Let the game start."
"Mind you Prem. If you lose you pay us three rupees."
"Ok! Let's see if you can stop me from smiling."

All the boys came nearer. Jawahar pointed to the tiger on the right said:

"It's all right then. You go to that one and I go to the other one."

Both approached their respected statues. Jawahar was the first to insert his hand in the big mouth of the tiger and then pulled it up with a smile. It was now Prem's turn who with longer smile put his hand in the mouth of the tiger allotted to him but while withdrawing his hand he started screaming. Along with his hand came outside a few yellow wasps. Holding his hand with the other one he continued screaming with pain and ran down the steps.:

All the boys started shouting:
"Premwa has lost. He owes us three rupees."

The wasps had bitten Prem on several parts of his hand. It was much later that Jawahar told us of the fact that in the early morning he had noticed wasps going and coming out of the statues, mouth and he knew that there was a nest inside.

The next day our picnic party was a real success and our miser friend paid the tiger's share.

Looking for the Swami

This is the story of my first play production and stage performance and it is also the story of the *Swami* who is the unforgettable character of the event that follows. It happened in 1954 when I was reaching my seventeenth summer. I had set up, with the collaboration of a few friends of my locality, a literary youth club. Its first members amongst others were Jawaharlall Phoolchand, Devcoormarlal Bhageerutty, Vidyanand Pandoo, and Hurrycharan Bundhoo. There used to be a long hall in the atrium of Maheswurnath Temple in those days with its three sides completely open. We had our sessions either in the hall or in the mango orchard adjacent to it. Reading of stories and poems from Hindi magazines and books and discussing them were the regular items of our activities.

Inspired by those literary discussions I succeeded in completing a full length play which I read to the members of the '*Ajanta Arts*'. Some of them were so thrilled by it that they asked me to have it staged. The title of the play was '*Parivartan*', the change. It was a straightforward story of a jobless youngster who got frustrated of his life because of the imprecation he had to face at home. The never-ending bitter moments of everyday made him leave his house. One day, while wandering in a far away village he came across a *Swami* who convinced him to go back home and to keep on his struggle.

After the casting we started our rehearsals in the Shivala's hall. In sunny days we would prefer rehearsing in the mango orchard. The main characters were shared by Jawahar, Nandan, Vidyanand, Hurrycharan and myself. I was also directing the play, an exercise never done before. On the day of the show, I had to look after the costumes and the make-up. Members of the club had prepared handwritten posters which made our show a well publicized one. We were expecting some hundred and fifty people to attend the show and according to this expectation we had gathered some extra chairs and benches from nearby houses. Our show was scheduled for 7.30 in the evening but people started arriving as from six o'clock and by seven the hall was packed to full. People twice the number had to stand outside the hall and wait for the play to start. The sight of the unexpected crowd increased the tenseness of all the artists. My friend Jawahar was the most panicked and went on asking:

"How could we face all these people?"

We were all struck with a sort of terror by the uproaring of the impatient crowd. I was giving a last touch to the actor's make-up who had to play the role of the ascetic. In the beginning, it was decided to provide tangled white hair and beard to the *Swami* with fibre of maize but then the choice ended to '*Lavoite*', a cotton-like material used in tailoring. The person in charge of the curtain ordered us to stand by, because public's clamouring was rising to a crescendo. It took me a whole hour to convert Hareea into a real looking *Swami*. My body was covered with cold perspiration and my heart was pounding. Children had started peeping through the curtain's holes. It was the temple's *Pujari* who, with his kind words, encouraged us. It was as though we were getting ready to fight a crusade. We were told that more than three thousand people had come to see our performance. The last advice of the priest was, "Play your parts fearlessly."

The curtain was to be lifted and I was the first to appear. When my father had come to know to my putting up a play he had scolded me:

"What a jabbering you are involved in?"

Before the starting of the drama, I was informed that my father was sitting in the front row with my mother and sister. It made my task more difficult and my heart started pounding faster. It never came to my mind, during the preparation of the play, that the performance was to be so hard a nut to crack. I held up my head. The curtain was withdrawn. Clapping of hands started. And the play was on.

But the real drama had to start only after the I fall of the curtain. Hurrycharan Bundhoo was so impressing, real looking in his *Swami's* saffron garb, his make-up so full of credibility and he was so convincing in his acting that at the end of the play another unexpected event did take place. A large part of the crowd stayed to see the *Swami* come out. Everyone was eager to meet him in person. Some of the audience were just waiting to congratulate him for his marvellous acting but there were others who were impatient to have the "*Darshan*" of the ascetic, to pay him their respect, because they had taken him for a real *Swami*. There were many of them who did attend a drama show for the first time; for them it was the 'great happening'. Even among the children a harum-scarum had started.

Harreea was still in his saffron garb but he had got rid of his beard and wig. Having provoked the belief of a genuine *Swami* among the village folks, he could not afford to come in front of them as a fake one and for me it was impossible to give him the same make-up, the same look. However, we all the artists did manage to free ourselves from the crowd and were back home. We had thought that after knowing the truth about the reality of stage and actors the folk would have a long laugh at themselves but that was not the case. A few of them went up to the extent of calling upon the actors next morning in order to meet the *Swami*. We were all asked about his whereabouts:

"Did he come really from India?"

(The rumour had it that way.)

"At whose place is he staying?"

This went on for a whole week. It took time for them to believe that it was Hareea who was in the guise of the ascetic. Yet there are among them folks who still regret of not meeting the sage in person. All those who attended the show have not forgotten the memorable *Swami*. On the other hand Hurrycharan Bundhoo, the *Swami*, though far from Triolet now working in a tea plantation, continues to talk of his great reminiscence of his life whenever he is amongst his friends of childhood.

My Friend Gaffoor

À travers a friend's own story is told and through it comes the story time. Therefore like all events and situations this autobiographical piece also *à travers* my friend Gaffoor is my story as well as that of time. Gaffoor was never sent to school and yet he was full of wit and was more intelligent than my friends. He was as witty as humorous and a philosopher in his own style whose utterances were sometimes beyond our standing. He had to join the sugarcane fields in a much young age than me. Once when because of his prodigal-in-expenditure habit he was advised to save some of his earnings for the future he said by jingling the coins in his hand:

"He who made these coins round wasn't a fool. The shape itself indicates that the coin is made to go on rolling. He who tries to run after this fast runner is bound to have his limbs fractured."

At that moment, very like my friends, I wasn't able to understand the meaning of what was said by the ever jovial Gaffoor. It was much later after brooding over the saying, that I came to know of his sagacity. Once again when I asked him not to squander away his hard-earned money on friends he said seriously:

"What's the use of amassing? They will be of no use to me after a few years."

I came to understand the real meaning of these two sentences some five years later when I was informed of his death. It was then that I did realize of the wanton and carefree way of his living. Despite his happy-go-lucky life he had all the time in him a certain depth unfathomed by us. Though he was the youngest in the group he used to behave amongst all his friends like an elder brother. Of the two reminiscences following here one is prior to his involvement with the widow who was twice his age. The second event is of after his addiction to alcohol.

At the time of the first event houses in villages were mostly of thatched roofs and conflagration was a common incident. Sooka's house wasn't too far from our house which on that day was incidentally on fire. My friends and I were playing "*Kabaddi*" in the open part in front of our house when suddenly we heard simultaneous voices in distress:

"*Aag lagal ba ho! Aag lagal ba ho!!*"

House on fire! House on fire!!

We had to stop our game and run to Sooka's house. When we reached there, there were already some people gathered in front of the inflamed house. A few of them were busy in their attempt to have the fire extinguished, others were just watchers. The fire had started from the roof. We, the children, were still stopped short when Gaffoor took hold of a bucket of water from the woman in front of him and poured the water on his body. We couldn't understand what he was after when instantly he jumped on the wall of the house and started sliding to the ablazed roof. He went to the part where the flames hadn't yet reached. Because of joint family the house comprising of four to five rooms was a long one. Members of the family had started crying and screaming. Sooka's wife was supplicating for her jewellery. The way Gaffoor was holding himself on the slopping roof of dried sugar cane leaves kept us all in fearful suspense. He shouted for water but because of the height it was impossible for those from the ground level to provide him with. Unable to get water Gaffoor took out his sodden shirt and started struggling with the flames. The blazing flames continued spreading because of the wind and became more violent. Somebody managed to get a ladder. The flames around Gaffoor roared. When the ladder was fixed a friend of mine, may be Bhim or Soonoo I'm not sure of, climbed atop. I took a pail of water from a woman and climbed up to the mid of the ladder from where my friend was able to take the pail from me. I continued in my manoeuvre and Gaffoor was amply supplied of water from my friend on the top of the ladder. People were showering water from the ground to stop the flames reaching the raffia walls.

It was indeed very difficult to have control upon the flames because of the fire inclined thatching and the wind. I heard Gaffoor shouting:

"I need one or two more people atop."

The air was full of smoke. The friend above me complied

to the call of Gaffoor and joined him. I was also stimulated and with control over my fearful timidity reached the roof to be in the mid of my two daring friends. People from below continued supplying us with water. When I was closer to the roaring flames Gaffoor asked me to stay away and told me just to hand them the buckets. We were in a suffocating situation because of the flames and the vortex of smoke made our eyes burn. In spite of it we went on fighting the fire. After half an hour of struggle we, with the help of a few other people who had joined us, succeeded in stopping the fire from reaching the inner part of the huge house. Influenced by the tremendous courage of Gaffoor it was my life's first hazardous move. In the evening my mother said to me:

"You are getting praise from everybody but, mind you, do not take such risk again."

Gaffoor was very fond of fruits. After wandering all round the forests he would bring jambos, guavas, berries and other fruits to share along with all his friends. Whenever my mother was to punish me for late arrival or other misdeeds and if Gaffoor happened to be there he would immediately come in between my mother and I. Once he had the slashing of the rattan rod straight on his face and the bleeding wound left a scar for months on his cheek. The second unforgettable event took place some four months before his death. I had my second car, a metallic Fiat Mirafiori. I was at the Esso filling station of Triolet for fuel when Gaffoor, an expert in climbing coconut trees, came to me with two coconuts in his hands. Without uttering anything he opened the back door of my car and put the two coconuts inside. In those days he was jobless and was living through the support of the widow. I was both amazed and pained to see Gaffoor, the most laborious of our group, in a situation like that. Once seeing him in his shabbiness I asked him:

"Why this flabby look and a beard that doesn't go with you?"

"It is the wish of Krishna. Very few days are left for this beard."

He was living with the devotees of "*Hare Krishna-Hare Rama*" in those days. I was told by one of them that Gaffoor, though being a very nice fellow, was an alcoholic beyond recovery. After having put the coconuts in the car he approached me:

"Let me have two or three pegs."

After having paid for the fuel I had only one rupee fifty paise left in my pocket. And of course it was the last week of the month. I fished the two coins out of my pocket and handing them to Gaffoor I said:

"I do not have more, you can at least get two pegs out of this. But please, Gaffoor, do not go on drinking in the early morning like this."

He took the two coins from me, looked at me and said with a smile:

"No problem. It matters less if you give me only two pegs instead of three but when it will come to give me shoulders see to it that I get all the four, my friend."

He went straight to the nearby shop. And I was left disturbed by his last sentence.

Hardly four months after that event I got the news of his death very late. Without losing any minute I left my office and drove back to my village. And yet I couldn't make it. When I reached his house his "*Janaja*" had left the village mosque and reached the "*Kabrastan*" of Plaine des Papayes. I couldn't give even one shoulder to the "*Janaja*" of my friend who asked me for four shoulders.

The Prediction

Most of my friends around me had started working at the age of fourteen. I had to do the same because of the dire straits in which my parents were living. But when my already fragile health started deteriorating my mother took me out of the cane fields. Even without the interference of my mother I couldn't have continued it because of the confrontation I had with the estate owner a couple of days back. By then I was reaching my fifteen. My long idleness would compel my mother to scold me by saying that all the boys of my age were earning for their living and I alone was staying at home with nothing to do.

It happened that one day my father talked to a relative of ours who was an auctioneer of vegetables in the Central Market of Port Louis. He accepted to provide me a job in his business and from the very next day I started working for Bhai Rajakarun. My only colleague was someone a few years older than me whose name was Prem. He was from the neighbourhood opposite the Kailasson temple at Ste Croix. I had to learn from him how to keep the book along with all the means and ways to collect the vegetables from the planters and selling them to the resellers of the market. I had also to learn the tactics of auction from Bhai Rajakarun. My work in the beginning consisted also of unloading the vegetables from the oxcarts and putting them on the scale before the display. For the first week I was given twenty rupees of which five rupees I had to spend on bus fare.

My father talked to Bhai Rajakarur for a second time as a result of which my employer lent me his old bicycle for a few days to facilitate my travel. I had to leave home earlier and was back much later. Once owing to a puncture in the mid way I had to walk for the remaining journey of about five miles with the flat tyre. A second time while returning home after the dusk I was stopped by a policeman and fined for not having any light. The to and fro trip of about twenty miles per day wasn't an easy task for me because of my not so good health but I continued with it for the reason that I loved the job. The only part of the job I didn't like much was the unloading and displaying of the vegetables.

In the afternoon I was free most of the time. All I had to do was to collect money from the vegetables sellers of the market or prepare the paying bill of the vegetables growers. The awkward looking office of Bhai Rajakarun was behind the stalls of spices and handicraft in the extreme lane. Not far from it in the other lane of stalls of *Puja* materials was the bookstall of Pandit Jadoonundan Sharma. I used to spend most of my free period at the stall. The first time when I was going through the pages of film magazines, *Rangbhoomi* and "*Chitrapat*", for long enough Pandit Jadoonundun said to me rebukingly:

"If you have only to go on turning the pages without any intention of buying, you better move."

But then when I continued going to the bookstall and showing my deep interest in the books and magazines Panditji got used of it and thus we became closer to each other. When I was casting a glance on new arrivals Panditji was busy advising his clients on matters of religious ceremonies and marriages. Within a matter of four or five days I read a whole children edition of the *Mahabharat* in standing position in front of the displayed books. After knowing that I was a relative of Rajakarun, Pandit Jadoonundun spent his free time talking to me very intimately. When he asked me and I told him the name of my village he wanted to know further and asked me:

"What's the name of your father?"

"Rajpatee Singh."

"You should have told me earlier that you are the son of Patee Singh. He is both a good friend of mine and a good customer."

And since then we became more intimate. The first two books I bought from him were Devkinandan Khatri's "*Chandrakanta*" and "*Akarshan Shakti*", by Gulabratna Bajpeyi, a book à la Dale Carnegie. It happened one day that in a jovial mood he asked me an unexpected question:

"How much do you get from Rajakarun?"

I replied after some hesitation:

"I was given twenty rupees the first few weeks. Now I am getting thirty rupees per week."

"And you manage to buy books for four to five rupees from that tiny income? People nowadays getting hundred rupees per week do not spend even five rupees on books."

Due to several months of draught in the country the vegetables cultivation was at stake. There was a big scarcity of vegetables in the Central Market of Port Louis, owing to which auction work ended earlier than before. My colleague Prem went to have a chat with his friends at the vegetables stalls and I went straight to Pandit Jadoonundun. After our closer relation I was allowed to enter the interior narrow part of the stall and sat on the old wooden chair which was rarely occupied but only by very close ones of Panditji seeking religious and matrimonial advice or foretelling from the *Panchang*.

Owing to the penury of vegetables, the market activities had become very slow. Rajakarun Bhai couldn't afford to keep me longer in the job. A couple of days prior to my leaving the job Pandit Jadoonundun spoke to me of his deteriorating health and his intention of closing his shop for ever. He was sorry of my departure and was full of regrets for not being able to carry on my daily presence at the bookstall. It was a few days ago Panditji was consulting his *Panchang*, that is his book of astrology, and forecasting the future of one of his clients when I asked him to tell me of my would-be days. He looked at me and just cracked a charming rakish smile on his broad face.

On the last day of my job when I went to bid him goodbye he took out two books from the drawer and presenting them to me said:

"We don't know either if we are going to meet again or not. These couple of books will remind you of me."

I took the books and brought them closer to me. One was entitled "*Maharani Durgawati*" and the second one was "*Nirmala*", a novel of Premchand. I was happy for the gift but at the same time I was pained of the separation. My heart became heavy. Pandit Jadoonundun Sharma looked at me very observingly and then said:

"The other day you asked me about your future, your destiny. Your destiny isn't in this book of astrology? It is not even in the lines of your palm."

I stared at him with agony inside. I could see in his eyes a combined glare of affection and blessings. He said to me with his usual smile:

"Your fate is written on your forehead and in your glowing eyes. The books which you love so much are themselves your bright future. Books will bring you in the limelight and pave your way to celebrity."

I didn't pay any heed at the prediction at that moment but today remembering those sweet words of Pandit Jadoonundunji I have my head bowed to his regards. Whenever I remember my sad days, I felt a mixed feeling of sorrowness and happiness which perhaps gives me the courage of understanding myself more.

Slices from a Life

Today's slice isn't one of those especially written for the readers of this column. It is being reproduced here from a book of mine entitled "*Atma Vigyapan*" ("Self Advertisement"), published in New Delhi by the Prabhat Publication in 1984 when Sir Seewoosagur Ramgoolam was amongst us. We have been hearing these days a lot of praise for Sir Seewoosagur. Many of us had the pleasant surprise to hear so much praise for Sir Seewoosagur coming from quarters the least expected. Wind changes direction. The reminiscence presented here isn't a praise but just a remembrance, amongst a few that I have written some ten years back of *Chacha*.

The Voice of the Prime Minister

The crusader of Independence and the first Prime Minister of Mauritius used to be our family doctor in his days of medical practice. Owing to which our relation with him was a close one. In spite of the great cultural influence of Pandit Bissoondoyal's Jan Andolan in our midst my parents' political allegiance was to the Labour Party of Dr. Ramgoolam. As a writer it was personally impossible for me to side with the ruling party. Despite all my respect to Dr. Seewoosagur Ramgoolam, who was my well-wisher, I always associated myself with the society rather than the state. Whenever, even from within, because I was in government service, I had to raise my voice in favour of the people's mind and against the system. I did it without caring of any danger.

One of those first instances was at the Youth Camp of Anse-la-Raie during the opening of a three-day Writers' Workshop.

The workshop which was to be conducted by three eminent writers of India—Dr. Vinay, Rajendra Yadhav and Majrooh Sultanpuri—was chaired by the then Prime Minister, Dr. Ramgoolam. I was forced by my frankness to close my speech in the following term—"It is unfortunate to say it here that this Hindi-Urdu Writers' Workshop hasn't got the expected help from the Indian and the Mauritian Governments." I had to put it bluntly because were it not the combined assistance of the ACCT and the UNESCO the three Indian writers would not have been in our midst.

No doubt all the guests and the seventy five participating writers were shocked when I said that we had to beg assistance from other cultural horizon because of the indifference of those connected with the cause. The distinguished guests and the participants all were of the same opinion that the Prime Minister was very angry of what I said. But when Sir Seewoosagur took the floor he started his speech with a smile—"I know that our friend Abhimanyu Unnuth is in a very complaining mood today . . . But then he is not wrong though he is often angry..."

This last sentence was indicative of what has taken place a few days back. It was at the request of the editor of "*Commerce*" from Bombay that I wrote an article in English entitled "*The Battle for Hindi*". A few Hindi teachers in the secondary schools were very angry after going through the article in the Indian magazine. They started a campaign against me because I said in the article that even to some extent the teachers were responsible for the pitiable and critical situation of Hindi in the country. The Prime Minister was informed of my crime.

After the Prime Minister's speech it was the tea time. Another opportunity for those angry teachers to reminding him of my misdeed. I was at that time engaged in a conversation with the Indian High Commissioner and Rajendra Yadhav when someone told me that Sir Seewoosagur wanted to talk to me. I went to him and he said to me, "These gentlemen are complaining that you are very prolific at writing against me."

This time the indication was to my editorials in "*Vasant*", the Mahatma Gandhi Institute's magazine, to which I replied very calmly:

"If I have to go for real hunting why should I go after rats and mongoose?"

Dr. Ramgoolam burst into laughter at my reply. Everybody around started looking at us and my backbiters lost their lustre. The Prime Minister holding his hand on the shoulder of one of them said:

"You don't worry. I know Abhimanyu and his family for a

long time. Whatsoever he is writing against me and the Government is one-fourth. If we try to stop him he will be going for four over four."

Perhaps this remark of Dr Seewoosagur Ramgoolam was bitterly taken by my friends as a praise for me but I know that it was the greatness of Sir Seewoosagur. It made me feel that despite my frankness I have never been able to say the whole truth. It is this sort of consciousness of an incompleteness that pushes me to go on writing. It doesn't happen always that the amiability of a Prime Minister makes a questioning writer aware of his right to question.

My First Protest

It is common belief that protest in the life of a man starts that very moment when he is born. The first yelling cry of a newborn baby has been accepted as his first protest against his being sent to a world not chosen by him. I have not any knowledge of my reaction at the time of my birth— did I cry or not? My mother used to say that I cried but my nurse, that addict of Hindi films, Madame Lebon, who all the time sang the same old song to me—'*Naina mohan prem bhari jadoo najarea*', I don't know from what film of that time— never stopped saying that I did not cry at all. I do not want to be branded as a non-believer by not believing any one of the two, and for that reason I consider that first protest of mine as an unregistered letter lost in the post office.

Going thoroughly down my memory lane I came to the conclusion that my first protest had occurred when I was being offered my '*doodh bhaat*', rice in milk in the imagined golden bowl brought to me by the moon. If my refusal to eat was not my first protest then it could have been the refusal to sleep at night after having fully slept a whole day, thus compelling my mother to sing the Bhojpuri lullaby convincing me of sleeping on the '*Chandan ké palna*', cradle made of sandalwood. All those could be mere presumption and my unregistered protests. The incident of which I was really conscious and which I still remember as though it happened yesterday took place some forty three years back and there is no doubt that it was my first real protest. I was hardly of nine years when the youngest among my sisters, Savitri whom we called 'Tiffi', was getting married.

The wedding pavilion of my sister was simply made of green bamboos without any paraphernalia because the heydays of my parents were gone. I had to sit by my sister on the eve of the wedding for the '*Haldi*' ceremony and without any objection gave myself to the ritual in almost the same way as my sister. I was having my '*Janev*', the ceremony of the sacred thread, without having any clear notion about it.

But the unexpected had to happen the next morning, prior to my sister's wedding which was scheduled for the afternoon. So the morning came and I was again in my yellow garb conducted into the pavilion, this time as the only main character of the event taking place. Prior to the customs and the practices of the ceremony of having the *Guru Mantra*, my first religious teaching from the priest, then proceeding symbolically to Kashi, the great place of learning and collecting alms for the spiritual teacher, I was asked for something that made me stand up from my seat.

I do not jut think of what happened next as my first protest but believe that it was consciously my first genuine protest. All the kins and guests present for the ceremony were shocked by my sudden objection. The first person who tried to convince me was my immediate guru, the priest, then it was the turn of my mother to explain to me that '*Janev*', the sacred thread ceremony, was also the tonsure ceremony and shaving of the head was a must. When I went on refusing to have my head shaved by the '*Nao*', the barber, my father in anger ordered me to sit down. Members of the family calmed my father and asked me to comply with the custom of the ceremony. The barber sharpening his shinning razor on his left palm was standing on my left ready for action. As he tried to hold my head I stood up again and came out of the *Maro*, the pavilion. The persuading continued but I remained adamant. I heard my mother saying—"Accept it my dear, otherwise the purification ceremony could not be considered complete."

I have to tell here that my family '*gotra*', the family lineage, was '*ichwakoo*'. The priest reminded me that I was of the same lineage as of Lord Ram and even Ram had to go through his tonsure ceremony. A clear indication that if Lord Ram could have accepted his head to be shaved then of what chips was I made to be able to object to it. Though I was nine I was not devoid of the elementary reasoning that after becoming '*coco rond*', that is after the deprivation of hair from my head I was to know the same fate as that of Chandoo of our village. All the children of the village had the habit of surrounding him. The tallest of them all arriving from the back used to close Chandoo's eyes with his two hands and the other knocking on his bald head with their knuckles. The cruel game continued until the arrival of an adult amongst the children or the crying of the helpless Chandoo. I did not want to become like Chandoo whose other name was Pingo. There was one more reason of my refusal and my protest against the tonsuring and that was my going to school with a bald head. When everybody tried to persuade me I started crying. With my two hands on the head protecting my hair I stood in the mid defying one and all. A few minutes back my sister approached me and said to the priest:

"Panditji! There should be an alternative in order to spare the complete shaving of the head."

The priest had a long discussion with my parents. He also talked to the other elders and then said to the barber:

"It's all right. I'll be reciting the *mantras* and you just cut some tiny pieces of hair from seven spots."

I accepted the last hour solution and was saved from being completely shaved. Despite my mother calling it the first sign of my stubbornness, I have to acknowledge it by all means as my first successful protest.

A Dream Created

There are dreams in life that disappear with the opening of the eyes and are never remembered. There are also certain dreams which are unforgettable and remain somewhere in mind for ever. But the dream being remembered here is different from both the flashy and the ever remembered one. It is an accepted fact that some dreams provide us the premonition of certain events that have to happen in the days to come but it rarely happens that a dream is imagined years prior to its happening. The strange dream which I am going to tell of came to my mind over two years before it was really dreamt.

I was in the fourth standard of the primary school. My teacher's name was Bissessur. He was a painstaking teacher who besides his good teaching was also very at ease with the rod in order not to spoil his pupils. And for that very reason we respected him and at the same time were scared of him. No pupil could have disobeyed him. Our classroom was away from the two main buildings of the Maheshwurnath Aided School of Triolet. To be more precise the new building was in the midst of the huge lychee trees and the "badamier" and had thatched roof of riverside grass. It consisted of two classrooms with ravelin curtain as partition. The mid space was always open to allow the charming lady teacher on the other side to have a chat with our teacher from time to time. On such occasions the pupils in our class were asked by the teacher to have their arms crossed on their respective desks and have a sleep with heads reposed on their arms. We were also asked to tell the class of the dream we had while sleeping. If this exercise was meant for a pin drop silence and relaxation it was also meant to provide a time for the intimate conversation between two teachers. It was some half an hour later that we were asked to lift up our heads and two or three of us were requested to come in front of the class to tell of their dreams.

It was my turn, on that day, to stand in front of the

class. For almost thirty minutes I executed the order and completed the so-called sleeping without any winking, without any dream. All the pupils knew that denying the dream meant no sleeping at all and the rod was ever ready for such disobedience. So when Mr Bissessur asked me to relate my dream I had but one alternative and that was the spontaneous creating of a dream. I instantly used my fertile imagination and told them of the dream that never took place. My teacher, after hearing with all attention, was pleased and said:

"What an interesting dream!"

Two years later that imaginative dream of mine was to become a real dream and of course with great bewilderment. Our examinations of the standard sixth were over and we were fully enjoying our December vacation. Summer was at its climax and the mango trees were full of fruits. The two trees at the back of our house were the first to blossom and for that reason they had the first ripe mangoes. There were of course several mango trees in our vicinity but "dauphine" was rare owing to which all my friends and other children of the neighbourhood were always around those trees.

I was alone at home. My mother had gone for fodder and my sister to a friend of hers. It was morning and my friends were not yet gathered. Dayanand as usual was the first to come to my place. We went together to the back where in between the breadfruit and the grapefruit trees stood the mango tree with the first golden mangoes. Beneath the tree was an old dry trunk of "goolaychee" which with time had become as tough as iron. My friends and I used to play horse riding and car driving on that trunk.

Dayanand was the first to climb over the "dauphine" tree and I followed him to reach straight on the branch on which I had noticed the two ripe mangoes from the ground: Dayanand was above me sucking the first golden mango picked by him. I moved from one branch to another on which I had spotted the ripe mangoes. After laying my first foot on the next branch I took the support of an upper branch with my right hand to jump forward. I had hardly taken away my second foot from the first branch to place it by my second foot when suddenly the branch started cracking. Before I could have been able to withdraw my first foot from the

Slices from a Life

second branch it was torn from its joint. And along with the branch I swung in the air and before the branch reaches the ground I was already on the hard trunk of the *goolaychee*. There was a sudden darkness around me and with great struggle I was able to utter:

"*Panee*! Water!"

In the meantime Dayanand was able to climb down and screamed for help. My *Bhowjee* and her daughter-in-law from next door hurried to me. After which the only thing I remembered was that one of the two ladies poured water into my mouth and then I was unconscious.

After a very long and dense darkness when I got the feeling of a hazy awareness a dim light flickered in front of me. I was to find myself in the midst of a vast plain surrounded by cane fields. I saw myself involved in kite-flying. A few minutes later I saw a dark bird coming from the mountain range and going round my head. The bird then flew higher to reach the kite I was holding by its thread. My hands started trembling and the kite went astray with the wind. I started running after the wayward kite which was taken away by the wind. I ran full speed with my eyes on the fast flying runway but despite all my effort the distance between us went on increasing. I didn't give up and followed through strange paths. I saw the kite reaching a flood of light in the sky. I was dazzled. Soon after the kite completely disappeared. I looked at the brilliant display of light at the horizon but its dazzling effect forced me to close my eyes. I screamed in despair. . . Then from a reverberating noise I heard my mother's voice:

"Doctor!"

And the next voice was perhaps of the doctor:

"He is back to senses. No need to worry now."

When I opened my eyes I saw my parents by my side around the hospital's bed. I looked at my mother and in a very tired voice asked her:

"Where am I mummy?"

"You are very close to me, my son. Don't worry. We are all with you."

After following the conversation of those around me I came to know that I remained unconscious for twenty four hours. Everyone was relieved for having me back and was involved in sharing the joy but my eyes were fixed on the

Slices from a Life

roof. I was still thinking of the dream. . . the kite. . . the dark bird . . . my running after the kite. . . the dazzling light. . . and. . .

And at the very same moment I was reminded of the fabricated dream which I told to my teacher of standard three and my classmates . . . It was two years back. . . the kite. . . the dark bird. . . the dazzling light. . .

My sister was talking to me and I was plunged in deep bewilderment. I still ask myself: 'Was it the fertile imagination of my mind that created the dream or was it a weird happening of life?'

Sold at Five Cents

My parents had known better days before my birth, even reminded to me up to now by whoever had known my parents in those good days. My father was then known as Babu Pateesingh instead of the abridged form of it which came automatically from the gone affluences. In their time of prosperity members of this family used to have not only their cariole but also their chevrolet. If my father was hijacked of his happy days it was because of the chevrolet itself but this is another long story. Let me continue with my own story—facts presented to me by my kins.

My birth took place when my father hadn't completely lost his riches and as I have been told by my sisters, the earlier part of my life was of days of a remaining pride. I was a child with a very poor health and no stone was left unturned to save me from all the health complications. This part of my life's reality was also told to me by my generous nurse Madame Le Bon, a great fan of Hindi films and their songs of that time.

I was born in the same place where I am living today, in the extreme north of Triolet, the longest village of the country from where the largest Hindu temple is at two minutes walk and the sea hardly one mile away, in the short cut. Yet I am neither a fervent devotee nor a very good swimmer. The silver beach of Trou-aux-Biches and the fascinating temple enclave were the only two places where I passed most of my childhood and youth days and the mango grove in front of the Shiva temple was the cool greenery amidst which came my first creative pieces.

I was the ninth child of my parents born before the family planning campaign, otherwise I would not have been born. Prior to my coming five of my mother's children, all boys, were already dead. It was believed that my mother was not lucky enough to have her baby son survived. Hardly two hours after my coming to the world, my mother, fearing the same fate to me, sent for a nearby relative of ours, Gossagne

Bhowjee, who came immediately. She was aware of the tragedy of my parents, particularly of my mother's agony. This village sister-in-law of mine (still living) didn't lose a minute in untying the knot of her saree and took out a five-cent coin. She handed it to my mother and in return of the price my mother put me in her lap. One of my sisters says that I cried when changed to another lap but my other sister says that I didn't cry at all. Gossagne Bhowjee after having taken me in her embrace had said to me (of course this too as told by my parents):

"As from today you become my son like my Vidyanand. I bought you from your mummy. I am no more your sister-in-law, but your mother."

I am also told that my first breastfeeding was from her breast. My mother, since her last days, was bound to believe that if, unlike my brothers, I survived it was only because I was given a second mother in the same way as Devki who after giving birth to baby Krishna was compelled to put him in Yasoda's lap. My mother's faith was irrevocable. She was reading the *Mahabharat* the days when I was expected. Like my father she too was a voracious reader and there is no doubt that I inherited from them my habit of reading. During my naming my mother listened to all the suggestions of our *purohit*, the family priest, but rejected the name suggested for me. She said to him that her newborn will bear the name of Abhimanyu. The priest could not accept such irresponsibility from my mother. He told her that Abhimanyu, the valiant hero of the epic, was condemned to live a very short life. He said it more emphatically:

"This name is not fair to your son."

"Why?"

"You already know that Abhimanyu died at the age of eighteen."

My father and other members of the family, very like the priest, tried to convince my mother of the risk of naming me after the hero of *Mahabharat*. They requested her to find out another name. But my mother remained adamant to her choice and declared:

"My son Abhimanyu is going to have a long life."

Ultimately I became Abhimnyu from that very instant to be later on deteriorated into "*Abheemanoo*" by the civil status officer of the colonial rule. Despite the tenacity of purpose of my mother, my father never called me by that name, which, according to a friend of mine Acharya Dharmendra of Rajasthan who was the first cultural adviser to our first Prime Minister, meant "the great anger". That is '*Abhi*' meaning great and '*manyu*' that means anger. In order to spare me from the fate of *Mahabharat's* Abhimanyu, my father used to call me by "*Umakant*" instead of my real name. Yet I was not freed from the definition of it because Umakant means Shiva, he who in his great anger dances the *Tandava*, the cosmic dance. My childhood friends who were not able to pronounce Umakant properly did call me *Makan*, and even up to now for a few of my friends I am *Macken*, a dilemma, not knowing where to go for my roots—Bihar or Scotland.

A very intimate friend of mine to whom I told this story of my birth for the first time said it in a serious and jestful blended tone:

"Now I see the reason of the impossibility of buying you. It is due to the reason of your being already sold at your very birth."

I told him that everybody has a price and it is death who is the highest bidder.

Religion and Spirituality

Goswami Tulsidas
- Sri Ramcharitmanasa (Doha- Chopai in Hindi, Roman Description in English) 1500.00

Ed. Acharya Bhagwan Dev
- Sanskar Vidhi 125.00

B.K. Chaturvedi
- Gods & Goddesses of India 150.00
- Shiv Purana 95.00
- Vishnu Purana 95.00
- Shrimad Bhagvat Purana 75.00
- Devi Bhagvat Purana 75.00
- Garud Purana 75.00
- Agni Purana 75.00
- Varah Purana 75.00
- Brahamvevart Purana 75.00
- The Hymns & Orisons of Lord Shiva (Roman) 30.00
- Sri Hanuman Chalisa (Roman) 30.00
- Pilgrimage Centres of India 95.00
- Chalisa Sangreh 40.00

S. K. Sharma
- The Brilliance of Hinduism 125.00
- Sanskar Vidhi (Arya Samaj) 125.00

Dr. B.R. Kishore
- Hinduism 95.00
- Rigveda 60.00
- Samveda 60.00
- Yajurveda 60.00
- Atharvveda 60.00
- Mahabharata 60.00
- Ramayana 60.00
- Supreme Mother Goddeses Durga (4 Colour Durga Chalisa) 95.00

Manish Verma
- Fast & Festivals of India 95.00

Prof. Gurpret Singh
- Soul of Sikhism 125.00

Shiv Sharma
- Soul of Jainism 125.00

Pt. Ramesh Tiwari
- Shrimad Bhagavad Gita (Krishna, the Charioteer) (Sanskrit, Hindi, English & Description in English) 400.00

Manan Sharma
- Buddhism (Teachings of Buddha) 150.00
- Universality of Buddha 150.00

Anurag Sharma
- Life Profile & Biography of Buddha 150.00
- Thus Spoke Buddha 150.00

Udit Sharma
- Teachings & Philosophy of Buddha 150.00

S.P. Ojha
- Sri-Ram-Charit Manas 95.00

Chakor Ajgaonkar
- Realm of Sadhana (What Saints & Masters Say) 30.00

K.H. Nagrani
- A Child from the Spirit World Speaks 10.00

F.S. Growse
- Mathura & Vrindavan, The Mystical Land of Lord Krishna (8 Colour photos) 495.00

Dr. Giriraj Shah
- Glory of Indian Culture 95.00

R.P. Hingorani
- Chalisa Sangreh (Roman) 60.00

Acharya Vipul Rao
- Srimad Bhagwat Geeta (Sanskrit & English) 75.00

Dr. Bhavansingh Rana
- 108 Upanishad (In press) 150.00

Eva Bell Barer
- Quiet Talks with the Master 60.00

Joseph J. Ghosh
- Adventures with Evil Spirits 80.00

Dr. S.P. Ruhela
- Fragrant Spiritual Memories of a Karma Yogi 100.00

Yogi M.K. Spencer
- Rishi Ram Ram 100.00
- Oneness with God 90.00

H. Seereeram
- Fundamentals of Hinduism 250.00

Books in Roman
- Bhajan, Lokgeet or Aartiyan (Roman English, Hindi) 95.00
- Hindu Vrat Kathayen (Including Saptvaar Vrat Kathayen) 40.00
- Chalisa Sangreh (Including Aarties in Roman) 60.00
- Shri Satya Narayana Vrat Katha (In English and Hindi) 25.00
- Sanatan Dharm Pooja 95.00
- Sudha Kalp 95.00
- Shiv Abhisek Poojan 25.00
- Daily Prayer (Hindi, English, French, Roman) 25.00
- Sanatan Daily Prayer 25.00
- Durga Chalisa 10.00
- Gaytari Chalisa 10.00
- Shiv Chalisa 10.00
- Hanuman Chalisa 10.00

Acharya Vipul Rao
- Daily Prayer 25.00

Books can be requisitioned by V.P.P. Postage charges will be Rs. 20/- per book. For orders of three books the postage will be free.

◊ DIAMOND POCKET BOOKS

X-30, Okhla Industrial Area, Phase-II, New Delhi-110020, Phone : 011-51611861, Fax : 011-51611866
E-mail : sales@diamondpublication.com, Website : www.fusionbooks.com

OUR BEST SELLERS

Come On! Get Set Go — Swati-Sailesh Lodha

This book is a genuine 'mirror' for you to introspect and evaluate yourself. It is not the run-of-the mill stuff dealing with success and personality development. It focusses on "Failure" and its various facets. Read what a failure is, does and think and then refrain from it. Your friend, guide and philosopher is here to motivate you and make you if not "The Best" but "Second to None".

Rs. 195/-

The Secret of Happiness — Jas Mand

Happiness is a state of mind of a human being, which is manifest in a consistent attitude of contentment. There are numerous examples in our daily life which illustrate that individuals with similar outside conditions have different frames of mind and hence varying degrees of happiness. It is not something that exists outside you.

195/-

Secrets of Success — Kapil Kakar

Thoughts originate from mind and by implementing those thoughts we get a result. In this book you will find at length about mind not only scientifically but also what Lord Krishna said about it. The topics covered in this book are the basics of life. If you don't have sound basics then you cannot move ahead in life no matter how much you pray. This book is for people of all age groups as it can help students not only to develop their personality but also handle academic stress in a better way.

95/-

IMPOSSIBLE...POSSIBLE —Biswaroop Roy Chowdhury

This book is about change. People by nature are status quoists. It is a state of mind. But those who are able to change, they succeed faster than those who remain tied to their old habits, mindsets and prejudices. This book will tell you how you can change the way you think, act and behave. It requires a little effort. But the results will be phenomenal. The chronic patients can recover, the habitual failures can turn around and the die-hard pessimists can become incorrigible optimists, from the author of Dynamic Memroy Methods.

150/-   125/-

For Trade Enquiries & Catalogue contact
Publishers and Exporters of Indian Books, published more than 1000 titles.

FUSION BOOKS

X-30, Okhla Industrial Area, Phase-II, New Delhi-110020, Phone : 011-51611861, Fax : 011-51611866
E-mail : sales@diamondpublication.com, Website : www.fusionbooks.com

HEALTHS Books

David Servan Schreiber (Guerir)
- The Instinct to Heal — 195.00
  (Curing stress, anxiety and depression without drugs and without talk therapy)

M. Subramaniam
- Unveiling the Secrets of Reiki — 195.00
- Brilliant Light — 195.00
  (Reiki Grand Master Manual)
- At the Feet of the Master (Manal Reiki) — 195.00

Sukhdeepak Malvai
- Natural Healing with Reiki — 100.00

Pt. Rajnikant Upadhayay
- Reiki (For Healthy, Happy & Comfortable Life) — 95.00
- Mudra Vigyan (For Health & Happiness) — 60.00

Sankalpo
- Neo Reiki — 150.00

Dr. Shiv Kumar
- Aroma Therapy — 95.00
- Causes, Cure & Prevention of Nervous Diseases — 75.00
- Diseases of Digestive System — 75.00
- Asthma-Allergies (Causes & Cure) — 75.00
- Eye-Care (Including Better Eye Sight) Without Glassess — 75.00
- Stress (How to Relieve from Stress A Psychological Study) — 75.00

Dr. Satish Goel
- Causes & Cure of Blood Pressure — 75.00
- Causes & Cure of Diabetes — 60.00
- Causes & Cure of Heart Ailments — 75.00
- Pregnancy & Child Care — 95.00
- Ladie's Slimming Course — 95.00
- Acupuncture Guide — 50.00
- Acupressure Guide — 50.00
- Acupuncture & Acupressure Guide — 95.00
- Walking for Better Health — 95.00
- Nature Cure for Health & Happiness — 95.00
- A Beacon of Hope for the Childless Couples — 60.00
- Sex for All — 75.00

Dr. Kanta Gupta
- Be Your Own Doctor — 60.00
  (a Book about Herbs & Their Use)

Dr. B.R. Kishore
- Vatsyana Kamasutra — 95.00
- The Manual of Sex & Tantra — 95.00

Dr. M.K. Gupta
- Causes, Cure & Prevention of High Blood Cholesterol — 60.00

Acharya Bhagwan Dev
- Yoga for Better Health — 95.00
- Pranayam, Kundalini aur Hathyoga — 60.00

Dr. S.K. Sharma
- Add Inches — 60.00
- Shed Weight Add Life — 60.00
- Alternate Therapies — 95.00
- Miracles of Urine Therapy — 60.00
- Meditation & Dhyan Yoga (for Spiritual Discipline) — 95.00
- A Complete Guide to Homeopathic Remedies — 120.00

- A Complete Guide to Biochemic Remedies — 60.00
- Common Diseases of Urinary System — 95.00
- Allopathic Guide for Common Disorders — 125.00
- E.N.T. & Dental Guide (in Press) — 95.00
- Wonders of Magnetotherapy — 95.00
- Family Homeopathic Guide — 95.00
- **Health in Your Hands** — 95.00
- Food for Good Health — 95.00
- Juice Therapy — 75.00
- Tips on Sex — 75.00

Dr. Renu Gupta
- Hair Care (Prevention of Dandruff & Baldness) — 75.00
- Skin Care — 75.00
- Complete Beautician Course (Start a Beauty Parlour at Home) — 95.00
- Common Diseases of Women — 95.00

Dr. Rajiv Sharma
- First Aid (in Press) — 95.00
- Causes, Cure and Prevention of Children's Diseases — 75.00

Dr. R.N. Gupta
- Joys of Parenthood — 40.00

M. Kumaria
- How to Keep Fit — 20.00

Dr. Pushpa Khurana
- Be Young and Healthy for 100 Years — 60.00
- The Awesome Challenge of AIDS — 40.00

Acharya Satyanand
- Surya Chikitsa — 95.00

Dr. Nishtha
- Diseases of Respiratory Tract (Nose, Throat, Chest & Lungs) — 75.00
- Backache (Spondylitis, Cervical Arthritis, Rheumatism) — 95.00

Usha Rai Verma
- Ladies Health Guide (With Make-up Guide) — 75.00

L.R. Chowdhary
- Rajuvenate with Kundalini Mantra Yoga — 95.00

Manoj Kumar
- Diamond Body Building Course — 95.00

Koulacharya Jagdish Sharma
- Body Language — 125.00

G.C. Goyal
- Vitamins for Natural Healing — 95.00

Dr. Vishnu Jain
- Heart to Heart (with Heart Specialist) — 95.00

Asha Pran
- Beauty Guide (With Make-up Guide) — 75.00

Acharya Vipul Rao
- Ayurvedic Treatment for Common Diseases — 95.00
- **Herbal Treatment for Common Diseases** — 95.00

Dr. Sajiv Adlakha
- Stuttering & Your Child (Question-Answer) — 60.00

Om Gupta
- How to Enjoy Sex (Questions-Answers) — 95.00

Dr. S.K. Sharma
- Tips on Sex — 75.00

Books can be requisitioned by V.P.P. Postage charges will be Rs. 20/- per book.
For orders of three books the postage will be free.

⬥ DIAMOND POCKET BOOKS

X-30, Okhla Industrial Area, Phase-II, New Delhi-110020, Phone : 011-51611861, Fax : 011-51611866
E-mail : sales@diamondpublication.com, Website : www.fusionbooks.com

OUR BEST SELLERS

WHY WOMEN ARE WHAT THEY ARE
Swati Lodha

This is a stimulating book on women. It is a book for women, of women, by a woman. It is a clarion call for the faceless, oppressed Indian women to wake up from the closets and come to the sprawling new world, where opportunities are beckoning them. **(Available in English & Hindi)**

Price : English–Rs.195/- Hindi–150/-

201 DIET TIPS FOR HEART PATIENTS
Dr. Bimal Chhajer, M.D.

This book is a boon for all heart patients as it answers all their queries concerning the ideal diet. Queries regarding diet–such as calculation of calories, composition and details about the fat content of various food items as well as what is good and bad for the heart– are answered in a lucid style and simple language. **(Available in English & Hindi)**

Price : English–Rs.150/- Hindi–95/-

Other books by Author
• Zero Oil Cook Book • Zero Oil Sweets • Zero Oil 151 Snacks
• Zero Oil South Indian Cook Book

THE INSTINCT TO HEAL

This book by David Servan-Schreiber, himself a scientist and physician, is a wonderful manual to help reconcile our emotional and rational brains. He bases his prescription about how to improve our lives on a profound understanding of how our brain works, on a broad synthesis of the latest knowledge in neuropsychology. (Available in English & Hindi)

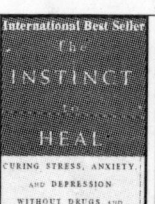

Price : English–Rs.195/- Hindi–150/-

ESSENCE OF VEDAS *Dr. Brij Raj Kishore*

This treatise is a compilation of all the four *Vedas – Rigveda, Samveda, Yajurveda and Atharvaveda* – in an easy-to-understandable language and simple diction for the common reades. It is a well established fact that *'Vedas'* are the oldest form of written books in our literature. *Vedas* contain the priceless teachings to human life.

Pages – 456. Price : Rs. 195/-

Books can be requisitioned by V.P.P. Postage charges will be Rs. 20/- per book. For orders of three books the postage will be free.

ⓒ FUSION BOOKS

X-30, Okhla Industrial Area, Phase-II, New Delhi-110020, Phone : 011-51611861, Fax : 011-51611866
E-mail : sales@diamondpublication.com, Website : www.fusionbooks.com